One Word From God Can Change Your Relationships

Kenneth and Gloria Copeland

JESUS IS LORD

KENNETH
COPELAND
PUBLICATIONS

One Word From God Can Change Your Relationships

ISBN 1-57794-199-3   30-0716

10 09 08 07 06 05   10 9 8 7 6 5

© 2000 International Church of the Word of Faith Inc. now known as Eagle Mountain International Church Inc. aka Kenneth Copeland Ministries

Kenneth Copeland Publications
Fort Worth, Texas 76192-0001

For more information about Kenneth Copeland Ministries, call (800) 600-7395 or visit www.kcm.org.

Contents

Introduction

One Word From God Can Change Your Life FOREVER!

When the revelation of this statement exploded on the inside of me, it changed the way I think...about everything! I had been praying for several days about a situation that seemed at the time to be overwhelming. I had been confessing the Word of God over it, but that Word had begun to come out of my head and not my heart. I was pushing in my flesh for the circumstance to change. As I made my confession one more time, the Spirit of God seemed to say to me, *Why don't you be quiet?!*

I said, "But Lord, I'm confessing the Word!"

He answered inside me, *I know it. I heard you. Now just be still and be quiet a little while, and let the Word of God settle down in your spirit. Quit trying to make this thing happen. You're not God. You're not going to be the one to make it happen anyway!*

So I stopped. I stopped thinking about that situation and began to get quiet before the Lord. And this phrase came up in my spirit...*One word from God can change anything.*

So I started saying that. I said it off and on all day. It came easily because it came from God—not from my own thinking.

Every time I was tempted to worry or think of ideas concerning my circumstances, I'd think, *Yes, just one word from God....*

I noticed when I'd say that, *the peace of God* would come on me. It was so calming. As a result, a habit developed in me. People would bring me issues. They'd say, "Well, what about...." And I'd either say aloud or think to myself, "Yeah, that may be so, but one word from God will change anything."

It began to be the answer for everything. If I was watching television and the newscaster was telling about a disaster, and the people being interviewed were saying things to the effect of, "Oh, what are we going to do? It's all been blown away, burned up or shook up...." I'd say, *"Yeah, but one word from God can change anything."*

It really developed into a strength for me and it can for you, too. That's why we've put together the *One Word From God* book series. There could be just one word in these inspiring articles that can change your relationships forever.

You've been searching, seeking help...and God has the answer. He has the one word that can turn your circumstance around and put you on dry ground. He has the one word that gives you all the peace that's in Him. God is Love. He wants to shed His love abroad in your heart by the Holy Ghost. He wants you to abound more and more in knowledge and judgment (Philippians 1:9).

God loves you. And He has a word for you. One Word that can change your life *forever!*

—*Kenneth Copeland*

Honor That Comes From God Only

"How can ye believe, which receive honour one of another, and seek not the honour that cometh from God only."
— JOHN 5:44

Kenneth
Copeland

Honor. Godly honor. It's the kind of honor that keeps its word and standard of integrity no matter what. It never fails— and it always succeeds.

Every day, commitments of honor are required of you. You have choices to make regarding ethics in your job, disciplining your children, keeping your marriage strong—and it's hard.

It's a choice between God's honor and man's. One brings true and sure success...and one brings shallow, temporal success that ends in ultimate failure.

So, how are you doing? Do you have trouble keeping commitments? Do people take you at your word? Or have they grown skeptical of your promises? If so, then you need honor—honor that comes from God only. You just can't live the Christian life without honor. You'll never be faithful without it. You can't be. Without honor, you don't have the power to be faithful. It's just not in you.

In John 5:41-44 Jesus told the Pharisees about honor that comes from God only: "I receive not honour from men. But I know you, that ye have not the love of God in you. I am come in my Father's name, and ye receive me not: if another shall come in his own name, him ye will receive. How can ye believe, which receive honour one of another, and seek not the honour that cometh from God only?"

A lot of ministries in our day have fallen. Preachers of the gospel have fallen. Church people have fallen. But I'll tell you something, you can continue to stand, and not fall. You can be a powerful force in the earth as a believer walking by faith. But to do it, you must be honorable.

God is faithful to honor you when you act honorably. That's because you are acting in something that originated in Him! He is honorable. When you operate in Him, you operate in honor.

Man's definition of honor, however, is quite different from God's. It is a derivative of the honor of God, but it is light and shallow—it is a false honor that deceives men. Honor in the world comes from men and is given to men in what I call "the honor game." In the honor game, everything is done to gain the prestige, power and authority that other men can give. It's temporal, short-lived and dishonorable in view of what some men will do to get it.

Take what happens at times in the military, for example. One man is honored by rank. He is given honor because he has proven to be a leader of men. The longer and better he does his job, the more promotions to higher rank he receives. Finally, he is promoted to general. Rank has privilege. It has honor. This man has come to his high position honorably. Men stand in awe of this officer, and they should.

However, some men who wear the marks of a high rank get them dishonorably—by scheming, begging or doing favors to gain approval. The only reason they want rank is so they can walk in money and pride and throw their weight around. That is not honor. It is dishonor.

These schemers have the same rank, the same "honor," the same privilege, as those who deserve them—but they did not come by them honorably. They achieved man's honor—man's way.

God's honor takes seriously the responsibility of representing Christ to the unbeliever. Peter exhorted believers to "[have] your conversation honest among the Gentiles: that, whereas they speak against you as evildoers, they may by your good works, which they shall behold, glorify God in the day of visitation" (1 Peter 2:12).

As a young man I understood this kind of honor. My father raised me that way. I grew up observing the kind of honor the psalmist wrote about, the honor of a man who "sweareth to his own hurt, and changeth not" (Psalm 15:4). I understood and respected the kind of person who did the right thing regardless of the cost—the kind of person who stood his ground no matter how tough the battle or how great the temptation.

When I was in my teens, my dad had an opportunity to choose to act in the honor that comes from God—or not to. I've never forgotten the decision he made.

A fellow hired my dad to work in an insurance business. Dad was very successful and soon made district manager. Then he went on to be supervisor of the entire state of Texas operations.

The man who hired him had been planning to start his own company. He had built up a very large amount of financial reserves while working with my dad for the big company.

Eventually, with the money and backing in place, the man announced that he was going to start his own company. He offered my dad a lot of money and a big chunk of the new company if my dad would come work for him.

By offering my dad this job and enticing him to leave the company, he violated his contract. So the big company filed suit against him for all those reserves he had coming. My dad became a key witness in their case. Their case hinged on my dad's answer to one question.

I remember watching as Dad took the stand. I wondered what he was going to do. There was a lot of money at stake for him. I remember how calm he looked.

"Did this man offer you a job with his new company doing the same thing that you are doing now?" the lawyer asked.

My dad did not hesitate for a second.

"Yes, he did."

I was amazed, but I was so proud. He just threw away all that money. He just turned down position, prestige, power—because he was honorable.

Later I asked him, "Dad, how did you keep from saying what that man wanted you to say?"

"It would have been a lie," he answered.

It was that simple. There had never been any question in his mind. His mind had been made up long before that situation had ever come into being. Why? Because he had already made a commitment—a commitment to be honorable. He had chosen to walk in the honor that comes from God only.

But Dad's honor didn't stop there either. No sir. Every time he saw that man from that day forward, he would walk up to him, shake his hand and ask how the new company was coming along. That man respected my dad for the rest of his life.

Choosing God's Honor

The world today often looks at the Body of Christ with a raised eyebrow. They've not seen honor. They've seen too much dishonor. But you can help change that. You can guard your manner of life, your conversation. You can be honorable.

The examples from the lives of my parents taught me a valuable lesson. I realized that honor is not hard to recognize. At times it may be hard to find, but it is easily recognized. In fact, honor stands out in the crowd because it appears foolish to the world's system.

To be honorable requires an act of the will, an act which triggers and releases all that God has provided for us. It requires a choice between God's Word and the subtleties and deceptions of the world. It requires a choice between the spirit and the flesh. It boils down to a choice between standing and falling.

If you are honorable, you will stand. If you are dishonorable, you are guaranteed to fall—and bring even more dishonor to the Body of Christ.

I get so embarrassed at what people try to do as believers, walking in dishonor. We are never to use our positions as preachers of the gospel or children of God to defraud anyone.

One time when I was shopping at a convenience store, a preacher came in to purchase some shotgun shells. He began trying to talk the clerk into giving him a discount on his shells because he was a minister. It embarrassed me so. It made me so mad that he would do that to our God.

It almost made me want to cuss so that clerk wouldn't think I was a preacher too. The clerk didn't have any authority to give the man a discount even if he had wanted to anyway! The young man got really irritated at that preacher. I wonder if that preacher has any idea how much damage his preoccupation with a petty discount might have caused in that young clerk's life.

Your Word of Honor

"Brother Copeland," you may say, "I see the value of honor and I want to walk in it. But where do I begin? How can I 'find' this honor that comes from God only?"

Start with God and His Word. He can make you honorable. He has already honored you with His own life. He has honored you with what the Bible calls eternal life, the very life of God Himself. He administers this life to our spirit man through the Holy Spirit.

As you get into His Word and allow it to get on the inside of you, as you allow it to become you, honor will well up in you so full you'll have no desire to walk in anything else. Your spirit will experience conviction about the smallest of commitments. You'll become so tuned to His Word and His Spirit that you will become honorable in everything.

As you become honorable, you will speak the truth. You will take your words seriously. You will never distort the truth or speak idle words. You will be able to make commitments and keep them. You will be able to be faithful. You will act with the utmost of integrity. You won't want to say anything else because Matthew 5:37 says all else proceeds from evil.

Next, seek honor from God only. Jesus did not play the honor game. "I receive not honour from men.... I am come in my Father's name, and ye receive me not: if another shall come in his own name, him ye will receive. How can ye believe, which receive honour one of another, and seek not the honour that cometh from God only?" (John 5:41, 43-44). The honor game gives each other "honor" or medals or titles in order to boost one's own sense of self-worth. It is saying you'll do something to please men, to please their ears. It makes vain commitments for fear of what men will think. It is a dishonor to God, however, to seek the honor of others rather than that which comes only from the Lord.

I made a decision a long time ago, over 30 years now, to walk in the honor that comes from God. I made a choice to stand on my word and His Word, and to walk in integrity. I made a choice to please Him and not men—at any cost. I made a choice to stand and not fall...and I'm still standing. You can keep standing too. Think about it. Pray about it. Then choose the honor that comes from God. When God honors you, what difference does it make what anyone else thinks? Your word and your commitments will be as good as His—He guarantees it. He's given you His word.

My Needs/Your Needs: Solving the Mystery of a Satisfying Marriage

Chapter 2

Mac Hammond

"If we say that we have fellowship with him, and walk in darkness, we lie, and do not the truth: But if we walk in the light, as he is in the light, we have fellowship one with another, and the blood of Jesus Christ his Son cleanseth us from all sin."
— 1 JOHN 1:6-7

Many centuries have passed since God introduced male to female in the Garden of Eden.

You'd think they would have figured each other out by now.

But even after thousands of years of living together, men and women are still a mystery to each other. And the depth of that mystery is most evident when they start trying to understand and meet one another's needs in marriage.

When men and women are asked about their individual needs in marriage, three facts always emerge:

Men consistently list the same five basic needs as being the most important to them.

Women also identify about five needs as being vital to their happiness.

The two lists are very different.

As we explore these enlightening lists, we learn the number one need consistently expressed by men was sexual fulfillment while the number one need for women was almost universally affection. And we find in the Word that these priorities were designed by God Himself.

"Talk to Me You Big, Handsome Man!"

The number two need for wives—second only to the need for affection—is communication—open, honest communication. Suffice it to say, husbands, your wife has a very real and important need for you to talk to her. I mean really talk to her. If that need goes unmet, problems are sure to arise.

The number two need husbands most frequently mention may surprise you. It's admiration. That's right, ladies. Your husband has a very real need to know you admire him. God points to its importance in Ephesians 5:33, "And let the wife see that she respects and reverences her husband [that she notices him, regards him, honors him, prefers him, venerates, and esteems him; and that she defers to him, praises him, and loves and admires him exceedingly]" *(The Amplified Bible)*.

That's quite a mouthful isn't it?

Be assured, ladies, the reason God puts such an emphasis on this is because it is so vitally important to your husband. He needs that admiration to function properly as the mighty spiritual warrior God created him to be.

Nothing will light his fire any faster than to have you, the woman he loves, tell him how great he is. When that happens, he will be able to conquer the world.

If you have a hard time finding qualities you admire about him, ask the Holy Spirit to show you his admirable traits. They may be hard to see right now, but they're there.

23

If you'll trust God to reveal things to you about your husband, you'll get so excited about him you won't be able to stand still. Don't let the enemy deceive you into focusing on what is wrong with him. Choose to begin focusing on admiring those things that are right with him. He needs it greatly, and more importantly, your relationship needs it.

A Lot of Truth...and a Little Makeup

Would you like to know what the third most important need is for most wives? Good old-fashioned honesty and openness.

Naturally, both husbands and wives need to be honest with each other, but this is an acute need for women. Every wife needs to know the man who shares her life is always being honest with her.

This is especially vital because it affects a woman's response to a man's authority and headship in the home. If your wife is going to be able to respond to your authority and leadership, she needs to know she can trust you. If she senses you're not being completely honest with her or that you're hiding something from her, she won't be able to properly submit to your leadership.

Take a look at 1 John 1:6-7: "If we say that we have fellowship with him, and walk in darkness, we lie, and do not the truth: But if we walk in the light, as he is in the light, we have fellowship one with another, and the blood of Jesus Christ his Son cleanseth us from all sin."

To walk in the "light" means to have everything open and visible—no subterfuge, no deception.

Only when we are walking in that kind of light can we have right fellowship with one another. Where there is distrust, there can be no true fellowship. So men, you must be truthful with your wife. She needs it. And as your God-given partner, she deserves it.

The husbands' number three need may strike some believers as being totally unspiritual, but it's not at all. It's the man's need to feel that his wife is attractive.

It's a rare man who doesn't want other people to look at his wife and say, "Wow, he certainly is blessed to be married to her!"

Now this may sound like bad news to

some of you ladies. You may be saying, "Hey, aren't Christians supposed to be looking beyond the outward man and into the inner person?"

Yes, but the scripture most frequently cited to support the position that Christians shouldn't be concerned about their outward appearance has been misunderstood by most people.

The passage I'm referring to is 1 Peter 3:3-4 where the Holy Spirit, through Peter, is instructing wives how to win their husbands. "Whose adorning let it not be that outward adorning of plaiting the hair, and of wearing of gold, or of putting on of apparel; but let it be the hidden man of the heart, in that which is not corruptible, even the ornament of a meek and quiet spirit, which is in the sight of God of great price."

Many people misinterpret verse 3 because the *King James Version* makes it a little unclear. *The Amplified Bible* more accurately says, "Let not yours be the [merely] external adorning" and the *New American Standard* says, "Your adornment must not be merely external."

Ladies, God isn't against your making

yourself look good. In fact, He's for it! He's just saying don't stop there—go further and make sure you've taken care of the inside too.

Women tend to be more spiritually sensitive than men. And men tend to be moved more easily by their senses, particularly their sense of sight.

Men are very visual creatures. It is vital that you wives not let your appearances go. It's important to your husbands.

I'm not suggesting if you're not magazine cover-girl material that your husband is dissatisfied. I am saying that you should make every effort to look your personal best. I guarantee it will make an impact on your husband. It will bless him and make your marriage stronger.

A Matter of Domestic (and Financial) Security

OK, men, now it's your turn again. Would you like to know what comes in at number four on most wives' list of needs? Financial security. You knew it had to be in there somewhere, didn't you?

Yes, your wife has a very real, legitimate need to know that the family's needs are going to be met.

All the needs we've examined to this point have had a basis in Scripture, and this one is no exception. Look at 1 Timothy 5:8: "But if any provide not for his own, and specially for those of his own house, he hath denied the faith, and is worse than an infidel."

That's mighty heavy stuff, guys. God's Word makes it clear that it is your solemn, God-given responsibility to make sure that your family is financially secure.

Many problems in our society today can be traced to women having to work to help make ends meet. Notice I said having to work.

It's the source of many marriage problems as well. Why? Because when a wife is forced to work outside the home for financial reasons, she faces potential resentment toward her husband.

So what are the alternatives to the wife working outside the home when the bills aren't getting paid? Well, praise God, there are some natural, physical steps you can take. And, if you're a Christian, there are also some powerful supernatural steps you can take as well.

In the spiritual realm, God has provided a way of prospering and increasing called "planting seed." We can tithe and give offerings and then watch God supernaturally work in our financial lives. I could elaborate, but I'll have to save it for another time.

From the natural perspective, you have three basic options when your income isn't meeting your outgo. First, the husband can work a second job or longer hours. Second, the wife can go to work outside the home and supplement the family's income. Third, and I believe wisest of the three options, is to reduce the family's standard of living to meet its current income.

Regardless of what steps you have to take, realize this, husbands: It is your responsibility to provide for your family. If you'll ask God to show you how, He will. He'll open the doors of opportunity to you, and then, as you become faithful in doing those things, more opportunities to prosper will arise.

Just like most wives have a genuine need

for financial security, most husbands have a strong need for domestic security. That's his number four need on his top five list.

What do I mean by "domestic security"? Domestic security describes a man's need to know things are being cared for at home while he's out hammering away winning the bread—that when he comes home his house is going to be in order.

Many wives don't fully appreciate or understand what it means to a man to know the home front is being taken care of while he's out doing his best to earn a living. First Timothy 5:14 speaks of this need: "I will therefore that the younger women marry, bear children, guide the house, give none occasion to the adversary to speak reproachfully."

To a man, a well-ordered home is a refuge. Having that type of refuge from the stresses and pressures of the outside world meets a very important need in his life.

Naturally, if the wife works outside the home there is going to have to be some type of division of labor around the house. She cannot be expected to shoulder the burden of maintaining the home alone.

But if the wife is a full-time homemaker, she has a God-ordained responsibility to make that home a haven for her husband.

Family and Fun

The last of the top five needs for wives is "family commitment." Family commitment means the husband has a vital, active interest in everything going on in the family.

The Bible teaches a man's family should be second in priority only to his relationship to God. You can see how much importance God places on family commitment in Genesis 18:19. There, in effect, God says, "I can bless Abraham because I know he will command and direct his children and his household in My ways."

Every wife needs to know that her husband takes ultimate and final responsibility for everything that concerns the family.

Men, that means sitting down with your wife and discussing the decisions that need to be made. That means establishing the vision for the family, talking about the discipline and education of the children, and generally taking an active role in the family.

It also means spending real, quality time with the children, as individuals and as a group. I'm not talking about sitting together in front of the television, either. I'm talking about real times of interaction.

The fifth need most frequently cited by husbands is for "recreational companionship."

"What on earth is recreational companionship?" I hear you wives asking.

It simply means getting involved and going along as he pursues some of his interests. The old stereotype of a husband always leaving his wife at home to go have fun with the boys should have no place in a Christian home. His best buddy is to be you.

He shouldn't have to go out with the boys every time he wants to do something fun. Get involved with him. Sit down with him and develop mutual interests. It will meet a very important need in his life and strengthen your relationship like few other things can.

Well, there you have it—the top five needs for husbands and wives. Put them all together and you have the unbreakable, one-flesh relationship that God designed.

As you learn to identify and meet each other's unique needs, you'll find more fulfillment, happiness and joy in your marriage than you ever dreamed possible. You'll discover the wonder of "being heirs together of the grace of life" (1 Peter 3:7).

Take the Shortcut!

Chapter 3

"Forgetting what lies behind and straining forward to what lies ahead...press on toward the goal."
— Philippians 3:13-14, AMP

Joyce Meyer

"It is [only] eleven days' journey from Horeb by the way of Mount Seir to Kadesh-barnea [on Canaan's border; yet Israel took forty years to get beyond it]....The Lord our God said to us in Horeb, You have dwelt long enough on this mountain" (Deuteronomy 1:2, 6, *The Amplified Bible*).

Most of us have heard many times about the Israelites' journey from Egypt to the Promised Land. We've read about how long they spent traveling through the wilderness. And it's easy to get the impression that the Promised Land was so far away it took years for them to get there. But the fact is, it was just an 11-day journey!

The Israelites spent 40 years making an

11-day trip. Think about that. They spent 40 years going around and around the same old mountain...until, finally, the Lord said, *You've been here long enough!*

I don't know about you, but I can relate to that. After I was born again, I spent years wandering around in a wilderness of defeat. I knew it shouldn't be that way. I knew God had promised me a life of victory, abundance and blessing. But even so, I'd still find myself stuck in the same old problems again and again, and I'd think, *Lord, haven't I been around this mountain before? What is the matter here?*

Then God would reveal truth to me. He'd say something like, *Well, Joyce, the problem is your rebellious attitude.*

Of course, I didn't want to hear that. I decided it was just the devil trying to make me feel bad about myself. So, I'd just say, "I rebuke you, devil..." and go around the mountain one more time.

What kept me in my wilderness was the same attitude that kept the Israelites in theirs. The Israelites thought their enemies were keeping them out of the Promised Land (and so did I). But it wasn't their enemies. It was their wrong mind-sets and wilderness mentalities.

Don't Look Back

As I studied the Israelites' wilderness journey, the Lord showed me 10 mind-sets they had which can also keep us out of our promised land. The first is the belief that: *My future is based on my past and my present.*

I'm quite familiar with this mentality. For years I thought that because I was sexually abused as a child, I could never really be successful or have peace in my life. I thought I would never be totally free in relationships. But that was a lie from the pit of hell.

The devil wanted me to think that what happened to me in the past would follow me wherever I went. He reminded me of my childhood. He reminded me of mistakes I'd made. Then he'd say, "Your life is ruined. It will never be the way you want it to be. You'll just have to limp along from now on."

But I've learned to reject those

37

thoughts. I've learned to say, "No, devil! God has a good plan for my life, and no matter what happened to me in the past, no matter what's going on right now, *I am heading for the promised land!*"

The Israelites, however, couldn't say those words because they weren't looking toward the Promised Land—they were always looking back toward Egypt. They said things like, "Would that we had died in Egypt!... Is it not better for us to return to Egypt?... Let us choose a captain and return to Egypt" (Numbers 14:2-4, *The Amplified Bible*).

God wanted the Israelites to come out of Egypt and never think about it again, and He wants us to do the same thing. So stop thinking about your past. Open your Bible and get a positive vision and direction for your life. Then, as Philippians 3 says, "Forgetting what lies behind and straining forward to what lies ahead...press on toward the goal" (verses 13-14, *The Amplified Bible*).

It doesn't matter how badly you've been burned by circumstances in your life, God can gather up the ashes and turn them into beauty (see Isaiah 61:3). And He will do it, too! He can even take what Satan intended for your harm and turn it around for your good. He can make your life so glorious it will amaze and bless everyone.

So turn your face toward God—and don't look back!

Wishbone...or Backbone?

Wilderness mentality number two is the lazy, apathetic mind-set that says: *Somebody do it for me. I don't want to take the responsibility.* This attitude is found in people who want to enjoy the land of promise without doing what it takes to get there.

You know, sometimes we have a whole lot of wishbone, but not much backbone. It takes backbone to do what God has called us to do. It takes work. It takes a willingness to grow to a place of maturity. Maturity is doing the right thing even when no one is looking. It's being like the ant in Proverbs 6:6-8 who works even though he has no supervisor.

Sometimes people look at the ministry

God has blessed me with and they wish God would give them a ministry like this. They think it would be fun to be on radio and television talking about Jesus—and it is. I'm blessed! But God didn't start training me for this ministry by setting me in front of a couple of thousand people. He started training me at the grocery store.

Years ago, when I had a bunch of kids and nobody knew who I was, God started teaching me excellence and integrity by dealing with me on little things, like putting my grocery cart back in the rack instead of leaving it in the parking lot to chase somebody's car around. That may sound funny, but, the fact is, it took time and effort to put the cart back. What's more, no one was going to come up afterward and tell me how wonderful I was for doing it. But by obeying God in little areas like that, I inched my way toward the ministry He'd promised me.

Do you remember the account of the sick man who lay by the pool of Bethesda waiting for the angel to stir the water so that he could get in and be healed? Personally, I believe that man had trouble with the

"Somebody do it for me" mentality.

John 5:5 says he'd been sick for 38 years. (That's almost as long as the Israelites were in the wilderness.) When Jesus saw him there by the pool, He asked the man a very interesting question: "Do you want to become well? [Are you really in earnest about getting well?] [And] The invalid answered, Sir, I have nobody when the water is moving to put me into the pool..." (verses 6-7, *The Amplified Bible*). In other words, the guy said, "Poor me. I don't have anybody to do it for me."

Think about that for a moment. It would seem that in 38 years the guy could have at least wiggled over to that pool! Even if he only moved an inch at a time, he'd eventually get to the edge so that when the water was stirred, he could just roll in and say, "Sink or swim, Lord, here I come. You're either going to heal me or I'm going to drown!"

That's the kind of attitude that man should have had—and that's the kind of attitude you need, too, if you plan to make it. No matter how far you are from the border of your promised land, just start where you are and determine to keep moving, inching forward as much as you can and trusting God to give you the grace to get all the way there. He'll do it. I guarantee it.

"It's So Hard!"

"But wait a minute," you say, "that sounds hard."

You're right...and that brings us to the third wilderness mentality. It's what I call the whiner mind-set. It says: *Please make everything easy for me. I just can't take it if things are too hard.*

I'd like to say I've been immune to at least one of these mentalities, but I've suffered from them all, and this one is no exception. I used to tell God constantly how difficult it was to obey Him. I'd say, "Lord, I know what You're telling me to do, but it's s-o-ɔ-o h-a-r-d!"

Finally one day, after years of that, the Holy Ghost said, *Joyce, would you just shut that up! All you're doing is making it worse for yourself. Every time you confess how hard it is, the power of your words makes it even harder!*

Since then, I've noticed how many people come to the altar for prayer, and I'll give them a scripture or a word from the Lord and they'll say, "God has already told me that...but it's just so hard."

Most times when we run to people for answers, it's not because we can't hear from God. We already know what He's saying to us. We're just hoping someone will tell us a way to get around the hard part. But that's not going to happen.

God wants us to go through the hard places, not around them! In Exodus we see that He took the Israelites the hard way on purpose. It says God could have led them by a shorter route, but He led them right up to the Red Sea instead because He knew they were not yet ready for war. They needed time in the wilderness to practice conquering the small stuff, like believing God for their basic needs, so they'd be prepared for the big battles that came when they crossed over into the Promised Land and really started confronting the enemy.

This is something people don't want to hear, but we have to hear it. Some things can only be learned in the hard times! If we want God to promote us, we have to let Him take us through a few hard times on the way. We have to learn how to go through those times victoriously before we can move on, because every time we reach a new level, we face a new devil.

Remember that. New level—new devil!

You see, positionally we inherited every blessing of God through Jesus' blood the moment we were born again. But we can only experience those blessings as we grow up and prove we can handle them. For example, I knew I was called to have a radio and television ministry for years, but no matter how hard I prayed and begged God, He wouldn't open the door for me to step into that ministry.

Do you know what He was doing during those years? He was building character in me. I could have preached just as well 20 years ago as I preach today because God has put that gift in me. But I needed more than just "charisma." I needed character.

That's why we don't need to hurry ahead of God in these areas. Even if we know we're gifted, even if we know we're called, we need to wait on His timing. Why? Because your gift can take you where your character can't keep you. And it's a shame when that happens because if you're gifted enough to help a million people, you can hurt that same million if you turn out to be a mess in front of them.

When I was first called to ministry, I had a lot of rebellion in my soul that I didn't even know was there. I had an uncontrollable temper. I was judgmental, critical and had an abundance of bad attitudes. When God started working on those areas, I thought I would die. I can remember occasions when I lay on my office floor and held onto the legs of my desk because of the pain that was ripping through my soul.

Due to the way I'd grown up, I had a terrible problem with submission. I hated the very idea of it. But God told me, *If you think this ministry is going to grow while you're rebellious toward your husband, you have another thought coming. You're going to treat him with respect and talk to him right. You are going to submit in the proper way.*

I want you to know that caused me some

real pain. I was tempted to run away from that word from God, just to alleviate the discomfort it caused. But I didn't. I decided instead to let God do a work in my soul, and you need to make the same decision.

"But, Joyce, that's hard!"

Don't say that! Get in agreement with the Word of God. It says, "This commandment which I command you this day is not too difficult for you" (Deuteronomy 30:11, *The Amplified Bible*). When God tells you to do something that seems too difficult, say, "Lord, if this is what You're telling me to do, then I can do it. I don't know how I'm going to do it. I don't feel like I can do it. My flesh would rather not do it. But I'm putting myself in agreement with You and saying, *'I can do it!'*"

Don't Complain

Once you say those words, you may need to be quiet for a while because the pressure you feel during those hard times will often push you toward wilderness mentality number four: *faultfinding and complaining*.

Complaining is equivalent to praising

the devil. It's taking what the devil is doing and magnifying it by talking about it. And just as praising God opens the door for His goodness to manifest in your life, praising the devil opens the door for destruction. First Corinthians 10:9-10 confirms that. It says: "We should not tempt the Lord [try His patience, become a trial to Him, critically appraise Him, and exploit His goodness] as some of them did—and were killed by poisonous serpents; nor discontentedly complain as some of them did—and were put out of the way entirely by the destroyer" *(The Amplified Bible)*.

Like it or not, there is a certain amount of suffering we must all go through during our journey to the promised land. (When I say suffering, I'm not talking about things like sickness or poverty. I'm talking about the emotional discomfort that results when God tells us to do things we don't want to do.) Jesus Himself suffered—but He suffered gloriously. Most of us suffer grotesquely!

What does it mean to suffer gloriously? It means to suffer without complaint. To say, "God, I trust You. I don't know what's happening here. This hurts. It's disappointing. But I trust You to bring me through in victory."

The best thing to do during such times is shut your mouth. That's what Jesus did. Right before His crucifixion, He told His disciples, "Hereafter I will not talk much with you: for the prince of this world cometh, and hath nothing in me" (John 14:30). He had enough sense to know that His mind and emotions were going to be under pressure—so much pressure that He would sweat drops of blood when He resisted it. He'd be tempted to say things He shouldn't.

We need to be quiet in the hard times for the same reason. We need to obey the instructions in Philippians 2:14: "Do all things without grumbling and faultfinding and complaining" *(The Amplified Bible)*. When you're able to do that, you'll be ready for promotion.

Remember this: The Israelites complained and remained. Jesus praised and was raised. So stop complaining and start praising. When you do, you'll speed your way to the promised land!

The Manipulator

"Let no man deceive you with vain [or empty, meaningless] words."

— EPHESIANS 5:6

Mac Hammond

Manipulation isn't easy to identify, and we can destroy relationships without knowing it. Don't be deceived!

If you look up the word *manipulation* in Webster's dictionary, you'll find it basically means "to try to control someone by deceptive means." The Bible doesn't actually use the word *manipulation,* but it talks about it a lot.

For example, Ephesians 4:14 says, "That we henceforth be no more children, tossed to and fro, and carried about with every wind of doctrine, by the sleight of men, and cunning craftiness, whereby they lie in wait to deceive." Notice the word *deceive.* It's an ingredient of manipulation.

Paul warns us in Ephesians 5:6, "Let no

man deceive you with vain [or empty, meaningless] words."

The reason manipulators use deception to cover up their motives is they think they'll never get what they want if they really level with people. Meanwhile, people they manipulate end up feeling confusion, anger, frustration and resentment, and may not even realize they're being manipulated. If the manipulation continues, trust will turn to distrust, and the relationship will collapse.

Friend, here's where we need to take a hint from God. He doesn't impose on our free wills because He knows the truth—that we can't change people. All the manipulation in the world can't change people, because real, lasting change happens in our hearts, and it only happens as a result of God's Spirit interacting with our spirit.

Now don't misunderstand me. It's not wrong to try to get people to do something. Nor is it wrong to be used by God to bring a change in them. But we sin when *we* make changes happen—when we manipulate.

To help you avoid manipulation, I want to show you three ways it surfaces in our day-to-day conversations.

Whose Baggage Are You Carrying?

The most common type of manipulation is the kind that imposes obligation on a person through condemnation or guilt.

When someone comes up to you and says you should do this, or you ought to do that, or you must...whatever—watch out! Those three words—should, ought, must—are three red flags warning you that manipulation is just ahead. They're usually followed by something the other person thinks is your responsibility. But the truth is, any obligation not based on God's Word is wrong—it's simply not yours.

An example of an obligation based on God's Word is to love. Jesus said love summarizes the whole law, and that covers a wide range.

Take your spouse for example: Husbands are to love their wives as Jesus loves the Church; and wives are to honor their husbands as head of the household. But when a husband hears, "Honey, you should spend more time with the kids than you do.

They hardly see you anymore, and they need their father," he's not hearing something that's rooted in the Word. You may think I'm splitting hairs, but I'm not.

Also, I'm not blind to the fact that his wife may be right. Nonetheless, she's manipulating her husband. Certainly he has responsibilities as a father, but she's putting guilt on him that will only stir frustration in him, eventually damaging their relationship.

She would be more honest with herself and her husband by saying, "Honey, I wish you would spend more time with the kids. I'm starting to feel like I'm raising them all by myself, and I think they need more time with you." See the difference?

There's another difference I need to point out here—the difference between condemnation and conviction.

A man recently told me that he wanted to change churches. He said, "I want to go to a church where there's not so much pressure to do this or to do that." I knew for a fact that the pressure he was feeling was not coming from the pulpit, though he was being challenged to live by the Word—challenged to tithe, to minister, to witness for Jesus and make disciples.

The pressure that he said was coming from the pulpit was really the Holy Spirit convicting him to obey the Word preached from the pulpit. Condemnation, on the other hand, comes from obligation that is not rooted in the Word.

Beware of the Tear-Jerkers!

As humans, our souls have three parts: intellect—our thinker; will—our decider; and emotions—our feeler. When we go through the process of making decisions, we use all three parts, and I want to focus on the part our emotions play.

Though we don't base decisions on our emotions, they do reinforce our decisions by rallying behind them and giving us that extra drive we need to stick with them. The Bible says if we waver, we will not receive anything from the Lord. So we need to be firm in our decisions, and our emotions help us do just that.

But when someone tries to manipulate us, they're actually trying to get us to base our decision on our emotions, and so they play on our emotions.

Have you ever been moved out of pity to do something for someone?

If you did what they wanted, it wasn't out of godly compassion. And when I say that was wrong, I mean *you* were wrong. Sure the manipulator was wrong, but you let it happen. You may have felt sorry for them, but if they keep it up, you'll find yourself feeling angry and resentful. And again, it can destroy your relationship.

So be alert when someone starts playing on your emotions—it's manipulation.

Sharper Than Any Two-Edged Sword...Careful How You Use It

God sent His Word to set men free, but the third type of manipulation we'll see uses the Word to put men in bondage when they use the Word against each other. It happens all the time and it must be a stink to God's nostrils. Paul addresses this in 2 Corinthians 4:1-2:

Therefore seeing we have this ministry, as we have received mercy, we faint not; but have renounced the hidden things of dishonesty, not walking in craftiness, not handling the word of God deceitfully; but by manifestation of the truth commending ourselves to every man's conscience in the sight of God.

An example in my own life is an outreach ministry of the church I pastor. We minister in our downtown area to a lot of street people. Sadly enough, many of these folks come into our facility with no intention of receiving the gospel. Still, they'll come in quoting Scripture.

"The Bible says you're to give to the poor. I'm hungry and I need something to eat. I need this...I need that." They use God's Word to manipulate us for their own benefit.

Another example that might hit closer to home, husbands, is when you tell your wife, "The Bible says that you're supposed to submit to me, so...." Then you go on to tell her what to do. You're manipulating her—you're using God's Word deceitfully.

You may think, *Yeah, but when she's off doing her own thing, how am I supposed to get her to do what I say without telling her?*

First, repent of your manipulation and don't do it again. Then, love her as Christ loves the Church and it will happen automatically. It will flow and make your marriage glorious.

Either Way...Love Never Fails

Whether you've manipulated people or you've let them manipulate you, either case is wrong.

How do you stop it? By speaking the truth in love—God's definition of good communication (Ephesians 4:15).

Love the people you've manipulated by giving them space to make their own choices without pressure from you. And, in love, confront those who have manipulated you. Tell them they're harming your relationship, but don't stop there. Take your love a step further by giving them what they wanted to begin with, if you can. Tell them you're doing it because you want to, because you love them.

Speaking the truth in love instead of attacking, defending or manipulating will improve our communication and build strong relationships. And that's our goal— to build the kind of relationships that God can use to minister to us and through us.

Getting Ready for the Glory

"Put away from thee a froward mouth, and perverse lips put far from thee. Let thine eyes look right on, and let thine eyelids look straight before thee. Ponder the path of thy feet, and let all thy ways be established. Turn not to the right hand nor to the left: remove thy foot from evil."
— PROVERBS 4:24-27

Joyce Meyer

I believe wholeheartedly that the major problem most of us face today is our own attitudes.

It's not the people around us who are causing us trouble. It's not circumstances or demons who are blocking God's blessings. It's the mess in our own souls.

If we'd pay attention to what's going on inside ourselves, instead of being so concerned about everyone else and what's happening around us, the Holy Spirit could lead us out of defeat and into victory. If we would just straighten out our inner life, we could burst through every obstacle the devil places in our way, because inner purity equals outer power. That's so important I'm going to say it again: *Inner purity equals outer power!*

If you'll read in the Old Testament about the children of Israel, you'll see that they didn't understand that principle. They always thought everything and everyone else was the problem. They never realized their own attitudes—or wilderness mentalities as I like to call them—kept them out of the Promised Land. That's why they took 40 years to make the 11-day journey through the wilderness.

But we can learn from their mistakes. By the power of the Holy Spirit, we can identify the wilderness mentalities that held the Israelites back, allow God to deal with those same attitudes in our own lives, and speed up our personal journey to the promised land.

In my studies, the Lord has shown me 10 wilderness mentalities to avoid. Let's start with Wilderness Mentality #5:

Don't Make Me Wait for Anything.

I Deserve Everything Immediately!

This impatient attitude is what causes us to give birth to Ishmaels in our lives. Ishmael was conceived from the union between Abram and Sarai's handmaid, Hagar, when Sarai decided to hurry God's plan along by taking things into her own hands (see Genesis 16)—and he caused a lot of trouble!

When we get impatient and full of fleshly zeal, we're likely to create something that's either out of God's timing or out of His will. Then, because there's no anointing or Holy Ghost energy to take care of something like that, we have to struggle to maintain it.

Remember this: Whatever God starts, He pays for. Whatever He births, He maintains. But if we get out ahead of Him and bring forth an Ishmael, we have to change his diapers ourselves for many years!

We can avoid such mistakes by developing patience. According to *Vine's Expository Dictionary of Biblical Words,* patience is a fruit of the spirit that only grows under trials. James 1:2-5 confirms that. It says:

> Consider it wholly joyful, my brethren, whenever you are enveloped in or encounter trials of any sort or fall into various temptations. Be assured and understand that the trial and proving of your faith bring out endurance and steadfastness and patience. But let endurance and steadfastness and patience have full play and do a thorough work, so that you may be [people] perfectly and fully developed [with no defects], lacking in nothing *(The Amplified Bible).*

Patience is not just the ability to wait, it's how you act while you're waiting. To be patient is to behave in a godly way even when under pressure. In other words, it's learning to be sweet and nice even when you're not getting what you want.

That's not easy to do. Although trials do bring out endurance and patience, they bring out something else first: ungodly junk you didn't even know you had! Pressure that comes during those hard times of waiting forces our impurities to the surface so we can see and deal with them.

Painful as that might be, it's good for us.

I remember one point in my life when every time I went to the store, I ended up in the slowest checkout lane. I'd get a clerk who was new, had no tape in her machine or had no change, or I'd get behind another shopper who'd bought things with no prices on them and I'd have to stand there while they hunted down each price.

I tried praying about it. I'd say, "Lord, now You know I'm in a hurry. Which line should I get in?" I tried rebuking the devil. But finally I got the message. God let me stand in those long lines on purpose because something in my soul had to be dealt with. He was developing patience in me so I could minister to the multitudes and be nice!

"I Act This Way Because I'm Irish"

Wilderness mentality number six is the

mind-set that causes us to blame our behavior on someone or something other than ourselves. It says: *My behavior may be wrong, but it's not my fault.* And it's often followed by excuses like, "I act this way because I'm Irish.... My father always had a bad temper.... I can't help it, I was abused as a child.... I'm going through a rough time...."

You can see this mentality of blame in the children of Israel throughout their wanderings (see Numbers 21:5). But the fact is almost everyone in the Bible had this problem. Take Adam and Eve for example. When they disobeyed God by eating of the tree of the knowledge of good and evil, they refused to take responsibility for it. When God asked them about their sin, "The man said, The woman whom You gave to be with me—she gave me [fruit] from the tree, and I ate. And the Lord God said to the woman, What is this you have done? And the woman said, The serpent beguiled...me, and I ate" (Genesis 3:12-13, *The Amplified Bible*).

In other words, Adam said, "It's not my fault, God! Eve made me do it!" And Eve said, "It's not my fault! The serpent made me do it!"

As human beings, we have a hard time accepting correction. We don't like to admit we're wrong. We like to believe it's the other guy's fault.

What breakthroughs we could enjoy in our lives if, when the Holy Ghost convicts us about something, we'd stop justifying ourselves and just say, "God, You're absolutely right. I repent. Please, change me."

Wilderness Mentality #7: Self-Pity

I have extensive personal experience with this mentality because I was abused as a child, and I reacted to that abuse by feeling sorry for myself a lot. As a result, I developed a tremendous stronghold of self-pity that continued long after my abusive childhood was over.

Even after I became a tongue-talking, baptized in the Holy Ghost preacher, self-pity was a way of life for me.

If I didn't get my way, I'd feel sorry for myself. If we didn't have enough money,

I'd feel sorry for myself. If I didn't feel good, or somebody received a bigger blessing than I did, I'd feel sorry for myself. Then one day, God stopped me in my tracks. He said, *Joyce, you can be pitiful or you can be powerful, but you're not ever going to be both!*

Honestly, I didn't want to hear that. I wanted to be powerful when I was in the pulpit preaching and pitiful at home when I wasn't getting my way. Pity had been my companion for so many years, I didn't want to give it up. I was so addicted to self-pity, I even set up circumstances in my life so I would have sufficient reason to feel sorry for myself.

Some weekends, for instance, Dave played golf on Saturday and watched football on Sunday. I didn't like that. I wanted him to do what I wanted to do, but instead of just talking to him about it, I'd start cleaning the house so he'd feel sorry for me.

He'd be in the family room, leaning back in front of the television having a good time, and I'd stomp back and forth vacuuming, slamming drawers and cleaning loudly so he would notice me. I'd storm through the family room to the kitchen. But instead of worrying about how overworked I was, Dave would say, "Honey, if you're going to the kitchen would you mind bringing me a glass of iced tea?"

That would make me so mad that I'd go to the bathroom, sit on the floor—I could have sat in a chair, but that would have been less pitiful—and cry and cry. "Nobody cares about me. I'm here all week with these kids and I work like a slave on the weekends, but Dave doesn't even care. All he wants to do is watch sports!"

Finally, after I exhausted myself, I'd drag back through the family room, sniffling and coughing, mascara running down my face, eyes all red and puffy, and Dave would ask "Joyce, is anything wrong?"

"No," I'd say in my most pitiful voice. "What makes you think anything is wrong?"

Any way you look at it, that's dumb!

But, praise God, I don't act that way anymore. I found out that I cannot change anybody with self-pity. I've learned just to let God change me. According to the Bible, if I follow His plan and do things His way, He will reward me.

I'd much rather have God's rich reward than satisfaction from manipulating people into feeling sorry for me. But there's another reason to avoid self-pity that's even more serious.

Self-pity is actually idolatry.

When we engage in self-pity, we set ourselves up as an idol, expecting everyone to cater to us and make us feel wonderful. Galatians 5 lists idolatry right along with adultery, fornication, witchcraft, hatred and other sins of the flesh (verses 19-21), so we definitely don't want to have anything to do with it!

Deal with self-pity by the power of the Holy Spirit. Stop focusing on yourself and start focusing on helping others. Take the flow of compassion (which you've perverted by turning it inward) and let it flow to those around you.

If you'll take care of others, God will take care of you. I know that for a fact. I tried unsuccessfully for many years to solve the problems from my past. But when I finally took my mind off myself and focused on seeing how many people I could help, somehow in the midst of that, I changed and my problems were solved!

My Way...or No Way at All

Since I don't have the space to write in detail about all the wilderness mentalities here, I'll just mention the next two. Number eight is what I call the dead-dog-and-grasshopper mentality. Study about the Israelites in Numbers 13 and Mephibosheth in 2 Samuel 9 and see if you can spot that mentality. It says, *I don't deserve God's blessings because I'm not worthy.*

The ninth wilderness mentality is one of jealousy, envy and comparison.

Wilderness mentality number 10 is one of stubbornness and rebellion. It says: *I'm going to do it my way or I'm not going to do it at all.*

Personally, I believe this is one of the most challenging mind-sets to overcome because it involves the will, and there's nothing stronger than the will of man. That's why it's so vitally important that our will gets saved.

We need to be easily turned by the Holy Spirit. If we're going in a direction and He gives us the slightest indication that's not the way He wants us to go, we need to stop and say, "What do You want me to do, Lord?"

I can tell you from experience, that's easier said than done. Years ago when I worked at a church in St. Louis, I was the only woman on staff. I loved my position. But on the day that church dedicated their new $3 million building, God said to me, *Joyce, I'm finished with you here now.*

Well, God was finished, but I wasn't! I liked it there. So I stayed for a whole year after that. I disobeyed God to the point that the anointing began to lift off my life.

I didn't mean to be in rebellion. I wanted the preaching and teaching ministry God had promised me, but I wanted it my way. I wanted it through that particular organization. I didn't want to go out by myself and start having meetings with 50 or 60 people in basements of banquet centers that still had crab legs on the floor from the previous meal.

But I couldn't do it my way. I had to do it God's way.

Stubbornness and rebellion must be broken in us. Sometimes when we hear the word "break" we think, *No! God's not like that. He doesn't break us!* And of course, He's a good God and He doesn't break our spirits. But there are fleshly tendencies in our soul that have to be broken.

He has to break the outer casing of our soul just as the alabaster box of perfume was broken (Mark 14:3) so that the sweet aroma of the Holy Spirit can be released through us.

Such breaking is a good thing! It will get us ready for the outpouring of God's glory. It will get us ready for new realms of blessing and prosperity.

It will give us the inner purity and the outer power to blast out of the wilderness and into the promised land!

The Defender

"But no weapon that is formed against you shall prosper, and every tongue that shall rise against you in judgment you shall show to be in the wrong. This [peace, righteousness, security, triumph over opposition] is the heritage of the servants of the Lord."
— ISAIAH 54:17, AMP

Mac Hammond

For some of us, it doesn't take much, does it? When we're talking to someone and suddenly it seems they're attacking us, walls go up and we get defensive. Right? Everybody does it. It's a natural response to any attack.

On the surface, that kind of response seems harmless—and even justifiable. *After all,* we think, *if we don't defend ourselves, who will?* But when we get defensive, we're probably more destructive than the guy who attacks us.

Wait a minute, you might be thinking, *if someone verbally attacks me and I try to defend myself, how can I possibly be the one causing harm—what about the other guy?*

We can't do anything about the other guy. We can, however, do something about our own responses. Understanding the wrong ways can help us improve in the right ways.

There are three common patterns that surface in our conversations, patterns that distort communication and cause relationships to end up on the rocks.

Let's look at four dangers linked to getting defensive, as well as steps from God's Word we can take to avoid these dangers. We'll also dig down to the root of defensiveness.

The Heart of the Matter Is Love

One of our deepest, most motivating drives as humans is love. We want to be accepted.

Our need for acceptance goes all the way back to creation when a God of love created us to be in right relationship with

Himself and with each other. It's no surprise, then, that rejection can be one of our most painful experiences.

Now some of us, especially we men, may be too tough or independent to admit this need. After all, it weakens our macho image. Yet even that is a defensive reaction to a deeper fear of rejection. By having a macho image, we hold back from relationships simply to avoid being rejected.

In understanding our need for acceptance, it also helps to face the fact that the world we live in is geared for just the opposite—rejection! Oh, the world does offer acceptance, but unlike God's, its acceptance is based on performance. That means if we don't meet society's standards, we're confronted with our failure and the possibility of rejection. What's so sad is, being the imperfect humans that we are, we're going to fail from time to time. And when we do, we get demoted, fired, kicked out, divorced, imprisoned...rejected. That's the world's way.

To make this vicious system even worse, rejection was all many of us heard growing up, even before we were old enough to understand what our parents were saying.

"You dummy, look at what you did!" Or, "You can't do this.... You can't do that!"

Rejection, rejection, rejection.

The result?

Defense, defense, defense. By the time most people are adults, all they know is defense. Even when no one's really attacking them, they get defensive.

So our tendency to get defensive is no great mystery, is it? We're simply beings who need acceptance, living in a world of rejection. This tendency is the first danger we must avoid if we're going to have good communication and good relationships.

Your Best Defense Is No Offense

Defending yourself may be the normal response to any attack, but don't be fooled. Taking a defensive stand against someone isn't right nor is it your best defense. In fact, it's downright dangerous and contrary to God's Word.

Another thing about getting defensive: You can always justify it.

"But did you hear what she said to me?

And it was a lie to boot! She had no reason to say that, and I was so nice to her last week. I have every right to be offended—bless God!"

How do we get out of this dangerous and deceptive tendency?

The answer is in Ephesians 1:3, 5-6:

> Blessed be the God and Father of our Lord Jesus Christ, who hath blessed us with all spiritual blessings in heavenly places in Christ.... Having predestinated us unto the adoption of children by Jesus Christ to himself, according to the good pleasure of his will, to the praise of the glory of his grace, wherein he hath made us accepted in the beloved.

Here's the acceptance we long for—the love we were created for. He has accepted us!

Friend, men's offenses and rejection mean absolutely nothing in the face of our eternal and unconditional acceptance in Jesus. No matter what we have or haven't done, we are forever accepted in Jesus when we accept Him and make Him our Lord.

Still, it's so easy to slip into our flesh sometimes and get defensive when we think someone is attacking us, especially when we're right. But that's when it helps to realize we're playing into the devil's hands by opening the door to division—the second danger to avoid.

Divide and...You'll Be Conquered

If no one ever got offended, we would never have broken relationships—no splits, no divisions, especially in the Body of Christ.

Jesus said a house divided against itself will not stand (Matthew 12:25). It's no surprise, then, that the devil's primary strategy is to keep us divided—divided in our marriages, our friendships and our churches. If he can divide, then he can conquer.

To avoid division, we have to get a clear picture that divided relationships, on any level, are an abomination to God. We are well out of His will when we're a part of division. And being out of His will closes the door to His protection and provision for us.

However, there are times when God says we are to separate from a relationship, and I want us to look at a particular one.

Romans 16:17 says, "Now I beseech you, brethren, mark them which cause divisions and offences contrary to the doctrine which ye have learned; and avoid them." God says to avoid people—even Christian people—who cause division. That may sound tough coming from the God of love, but here's why.

Verse 18: "For they that are such serve not our Lord Jesus Christ, but their own belly...."

Still, we don't have to get offended when people say something to us that could cause division. Amos 3:3 asks the question: "Can two walk together, except they be agreed?"

There's no way we can walk together and accomplish God's purposes unless we're in agreement. So if we'll just take time to ask the Holy Spirit, He will tell us what we can do to maintain agreement and avoid division. Once we really understand that divided relationships are not of God, we'll never allow ourselves to get offended or defensive, even if someone does us wrong.

He Who Has Ears to Hear...

Just as God uses people to minister to us, He also uses people to correct us. Here's where we find the third danger of defensiveness—becoming unteachable.

When we get offended and raise our walls in defense, those walls can block out the very words we need to hear, such as words of correction God may be speaking through someone. They're words that benefit us by causing us to change and grow. But if we're quick to be defensive, we certainly won't want to hear a person point out something wrong in us. If we continue to block out correction, errors in our lives will go unchanged and we won't grow.

That's how we become unteachable.

I came across a study which concluded that 95 percent of all criticisms people make have some basis in fact. I believe we can conclude that as long as we have hearts that hear, we can benefit from almost any criticism. Realizing this benefit can change our attitude about threatening situations and help us not be defensive.

Go Big "D"

So, are you wondering where God is in our offense-defense problems?

Well, you may be surprised to find out that all too often He's not in the picture.

Why? Because we reject His defense on our behalf, which is the fourth danger of the defender pattern.

You see, God desires to be our vindicator and recompense. He stands ready to defend us, but when we allow ourselves to be offended, we close Him out of the picture. We take matters into our own hands instead of leaving them in His, and we keep Him from being our Defender.

God promises that "every tongue that shall rise against thee in judgment thou shalt condemn" (Isaiah 54:17). It's our heritage as His servants. But to receive this heritage, God requires that we let Him carry the ball. We must roll every attack and offense onto Him. Though it may seem to take awhile sometimes, God will always show us to be in the right—if we let Him.

As we give our offenses to God, we

become less defensive and more effective in talking to each other. The better our communication, the better our relationships. And that's our goal: to build the kind of relationships that God can use to minister to us and through us.

"Till Death Do You Part" Is a Long, Long Time

"Let the peace...from Christ rule (act as umpire continually) in your hearts."
— COLOSSIANS 3:15, AMP

If you're over 25 and single, chances are, you've felt the pressure. Maybe it has come from well-meaning parents, overly eager for grandchildren. Maybe it has come from friends who think that because they're married, you should be too.

Maybe you've felt pressured by your own insecurities as you have wondered, *What's wrong with me? Is it the way I wear my hair? Am I too fat? Too skinny? Why am I not married yet?!*

If you're unmarried and starting to get frantic about it, stop. Take the next few minutes, climb out of the pressure cooker and take an honest look at what a mate can and can't do for you. By doing so, you might well avoid one of the greatest catastrophes life can bring—a bad marriage.

As a pastor, I can tell you that Christians are being trapped in such marriages all the time. They're marrying the wrong people for all the wrong reasons. They're being deceived by marriage myths that have left them disappointed, disillusioned and, all too often, divorced.

Myth #1: The Loneliness Cure

The first of those myths is the belief that marriage will put an end to loneliness. One single woman, sadly deceived by this myth, wrote:

> I can't think of anything I hate more than being alone. Everywhere I turn, I see couples. Couples on TV, couples in cars, couples on planes, couples in restaurants, couples in parks, couples...couples...couples. Everywhere there are reminders that I am alone. I wonder if I will ever find a person to fill that hole in my heart.

Child of God, if you ever find yourself thinking like that, warning signals should start flashing in your mind because you're expecting something from marriage that it never can give you. Marriage is not the "cure-all" for human loneliness. There are many desperately lonely married people who can vouch for that.

You see, God created human beings to yearn for two levels of relational intimacy. Granted, one of them is the yearning for an honest and trusting relationship with a friend or marriage partner. But the second one is far greater. It's the yearning to enter an authentic, growing relationship with God.

We've been putting too much emphasis on meeting a mate, believing that mate will fill the hole in our heart. But they can't do it. A mate might fill the space in your house, but they can't fill the hole in your heart.

Only Jesus can fill your heart. It's fine to date someone, but that person is not the loneliness cure. Jesus is your cure. So the dating relationship should direct both of you—as individuals—to an increasing intimacy in your relationship with God. As He becomes stronger in your lives individually,

85

then you'll have a completeness you have never before experienced.

In John 10:10, Jesus said, "I am come that they might have life, and that they might have it more abundantly." Remember this: Only Jesus can give you abundant life. Only He can give you a life so full that it puts loneliness behind you forever. That curly-headed cutie who catches your eye can't do that for you.

So before you plunge into a human relationship with expectations that never can be met, plunge into the depths of your relationship with Jesus Christ. Build a solid foundation in Him.

Myth #2: The Life Preserver

The second myth many people believe about marriage is that it will heal their broken heart. They're hurting and they think, *If I can just find a mate, I'll feel better.*

If that's what you think, then think again.

A man or woman who is drowning in emotional pain and latches on to marriage as a life preserver is opening the door for disaster. I've seen it time and again. One day the life-preserving spouse will stand up and say, "Please, can you just back off and give me some space?!"

Then the pain-filled spouse will interpret that request as another round of rejection, neglect or abuse. When they react to that threat, chaos will break out in the marriage.

Healthy marriages cannot be built on foundations of brokenness. Spouses cannot heal broken, messed-up hearts. Only Jesus can do that kind of heart surgery.

Therefore, if you're hurting, if you're plagued with feelings of inferiority and fears of being abandoned, don't cling to a boyfriend or girlfriend. Cling to Jesus. Develop a personal relationship with Him, and you'll find He can be the best companion and lover you could ever have. He'll never leave you nor forsake you. He's a friend who sticks closer than a brother.

You don't need that unemployed, cocaine-using boyfriend who's been using and abusing you. You don't need that girlfriend who criticizes and belittles you. Kick those heartbreakers out of your life and get hooked up to Jesus. He'll take care of you.

Myth #3: Happily Ever After

The third and perhaps most common myth to beware of is this: Marriage will make me happy.

Countless singles fall for that lie. They think, *I'm not content now as a single, but if I can get married, I'll be content. After all, I'll have my wife, a fireplace and a wonderful life. We'll get cozy on the couch, listen to Lou Rawls records and live happily ever after.*

You know what I would say to that?

Wake up!

An unhappy single equals an unhappy marriage. An angry single equals an angry marriage. A dissatisfied single equals a dissatisfied marriage. Whatever you are when you are single, that's what you'll be when you're married, because marriage does not produce life or character transformation.

Jesus transforms. The Word of God transforms. But marriage does not. It will not transform you and it will not transform the one you marry. If your boyfriend is a frog before you marry him, he'll be a frog after you marry him. Saying "I do" won't turn him into a prince.

Character changes are produced by the inner work of the Holy Spirit independently of one's marital status. Whether you're married or single, if changes need to be made within your heart, they will have to be made by meditating on God's Word, acting on that Word and being yielded to the Holy Spirit. There is no other way to get the job done.

Myth #4: Marriage Is for Everyone

Despite the fact that most people in our society eventually get married, it's important to keep in mind that marriage is not God's plan for everyone. There are those who, like the Apostle Paul, have the gift of abstinence. That simply means they have no compelling need for a sexual relationship.

Such gifted people can serve God in ministry in a much greater way than married people, because they don't have to attend to the responsibilities of a family. In 1 Corinthians 7, Paul, addressing this subject, writes:

But and if thou marry, thou hast not sinned; and if a virgin marry, she hath not sinned. Nevertheless such shall have trouble in the flesh: but I spare you... But I would have you without carefulness. He that is unmarried careth for the things that belong to the Lord, how he may please the Lord: But he that is married careth for the things that are of the world, how he may please his wife.... The unmarried woman careth for the things of the Lord, that she may be holy both in body and in spirit: but she that is married careth for the things of the world, how she may please her husband (verses 28, 32-34).

You need to realize in advance, some troubles will arise in your life as a result of marriage. You're living in a fools' paradise if you think just because you have a romantic experience—or even a spiritual experience—with your mate that you won't have problems.

Marriage is made of problems! It is a continuing opportunity to cope with and overcome one attack of the devil right after another. If you go into marriage thinking otherwise, you're already starting out on the wrong foot.

For that reason, Paul advises those who want to give themselves completely to the ministry of the Lord to remain single. Paul says, however, if they cannot abstain from sexual passion, "let them marry: for it is better to marry than to burn" (1 Corinthians 7:9).

But that doesn't mean you should get married because you're burning with sexual lust. No, fix the burn before you get married, because if you marry with the burn, you'll burn up after you get married! The lust that drove you to marriage will eventually drive you out of your own household into adulterous relationships. So deal with it now.

Take Your Time

"Okay, Pastor Dollar," you say, "I'm ready. I have built a solid relationship with Jesus. He's healed my broken heart. I'm happy, healthy and I want to get married. Do you have any other words of wisdom for me?"

Yes, when you choose a mate, be absolutely sure to obey the instructions God gives in 2 Corinthians 6: "Be ye not unequally yoked together with unbelievers: for what fellowship hath righteousness with unrighteousness? and what communion hath light with darkness? And what concord hath Christ with Belial? or what part hath he that believeth with an infidel?" (verses 14-15).

In other words, only marry a believer. Unpopular though it sometimes may be among singles, that is a requirement of God. Keep it without compromise.

If you're dating a man who is "kind of saved," who drinks a little and smokes a little and cusses a little, then get rid of him until he gets delivered from that little bit of stuff he's been doing. You don't need to marry into that mess. You wait until he gets "real saved" before you marry him.

Even then, don't rush into anything. Take the time to observe that potential mate very carefully. People are not always what they appear to be. Just because they say they're a Christian, don't automatically believe it.

The Bible says you'll know who's a Christian by the fruit they bear. So let that boyfriend or girlfriend bear some fruit first. Then give it some time to see if that fruit lasts. Don't say, "Well, he bore fruit last week, so we'll get married next week!"

No, I advise you to give it at least one year. If that boy is still opening doors for you and sending you flowers, if he's still concerned about you and hasn't pressured you into sexual activity after a year, reel him in because he's a good catch! If that girl is still talking sweetly to you and treating you with respect after she's been seeing you a year, set the wedding date, because she's the one you've been praying for God to send.

Finally, as Colossians 3:15 says, "let the peace...from Christ rule (act as umpire continually) in your hearts" *(The Amplified Bible)*. Next to making Jesus your Lord, choosing a mate is the most monumental decision you'll ever make. So don't do anything unless God's peace in your heart tells you it's safe.

Let Him direct you. Never jump ahead of Him. Relax and let God bring your marriage to pass in His own way. Don't get in a hurry and make a mistake. After all, "till death do you part" is a long, long time.

Love in the Home

Chapter 8

"For where envying and strife is, there is confusion and every evil work."
— JAMES 3:16

*Gloria
Copeland*

Ken and I have learned the importance of agreement in the home. We have learned through the Word of God how to live in agreement with each other and with our children. The power of harmony is at work in our lives—whatever we agree on according to God's Word comes to pass. We do not allow strife in our home, our office or any part of our ministry. *Strife stops the power of God.*

We have learned a great truth: It is more important to avoid strife than to appear justified. It is better to give than to receive. And the wisdom from above is peace-loving and easily entreated, willing to yield to reason. As a result, we are enjoying one of God's greatest blessings: a love-ruled home.

When you begin to order your life by the

love of God, you will find that the easiest place to remain in selfishness is in your own home with those dearest to you. There seems to be an incentive to operate in love before other people, but with our family we are tempted to allow ourselves more selfish privileges—as if selfishness does not really matter at home. The truth is, there is no barrier in the home to keep us from seeking our own, *except* the love of God.

Before we even thought about living the love of God, we were probably more courteous, and just nicer in many ways, to friends and acquaintances than to our own families. Without the love of God, we are more demanding and less forgiving with the members of our own families than with anyone else. It does not make sense, but most of the time we will say things to those closest to us that we would not dream of saying to other people.

Discord or disagreement in any relationship—husband and wife, parent and child, brother and sister—drops the shield of faith, stops prayer results and invites Satan and his evil spirits into the midst of that situation.

The Bible tells us in James 3:16, "Where envying and strife is there is confusion and every evil work." Envy, or jealousy, and strife—contention, rivalry and selfish ambition—are areas of darkness. Envy results in strife. And strife brings confusion and opens the door to every evil work. If we walk in strife, we walk in the wisdom of darkness and our senses dominate our spirit. Strife will stop us from perfecting the love of God. It will cause us to walk in darkness instead of in the light of God's wisdom.

Strife is deadly. It stops faith and paralyzes the power of God in our lives. The moment we become aware of Satan trying to move us into an area of strife, we must stop it immediately in the Name of Jesus. We learn to resist strife just as we learn to resist sin and sickness. Contention must stop—it proceeds from the devil. The Word says, "Let nothing be done through strife or vainglory" (Philippians 2:3). When we obey God's Word, we will be free from Satan's evil works.

Strife and selfishness are luxuries believers cannot afford, even at home—*especially at home!* If we allow the devil to stop us with strife at our own front door, we will be no threat to him anywhere else. The home is where strife is the deadliest. The home is also the place where living the love of God produces the greatest joy and blessings. Our home becomes a habitation of love and joy when it is love-ruled by the Word of God.

A Christian husband and wife who learn to live in agreement—without strife—are mighty instruments of the Lord Jesus. A Christian father and mother standing in harmony and agreement where their children are concerned *will* see manifestations of the Word of God at work. The rewards of living in agreement are more than worth the effort it takes to walk in love with one another.

Chapter 9

My Father and My Friend

Kenneth Copeland

"For ye have not received the spirit of bondage again to fear; but ye have received the Spirit of adoption, whereby we cry, Abba, Father. The Spirit itself beareth witness with our spirit, that we are the children of God."
— ROMANS 8:15-16

How much time do you spend fellowshiping with your heavenly Father? For most people, that's an embarrassing question. They get nervous at the very suggestion that a mere human being could actually fellowship with God. But they shouldn't. In fact, if they were getting their information from the Bible, if they were living and talking and acting like who the Bible says they are in Jesus, they'd be living as though Jesus is their very best friend.

Of course, if they did that, some folks would think they'd gone off the deep end.

I know because they already think that of me. They say, "Kenneth Copeland, you're out of your mind. You're trying to bring God down to your own level."

But what they don't realize is this: I didn't have one thing to do with that! He came down to our level of His own free will. He died and bore our sins by His own desire. I didn't have to bring Him down to my level. He came of His own accord.

I've had other people tell me, "You're trying to raise yourself up equal to God." But I didn't have anything to do with that either. The Bible says, "[He] hath raised us up together, and made us sit together in heavenly places" (Ephesians 2:6). I didn't do it. *He* did it! That's the good news! That's the gospel! I didn't have to lift myself up. He's already done it.

On top of all that, God Himself has said in His Word that He wants to get into a close relationship with us. First Corinthians 1:9 says He's called us into fellowship with Him!

Fellowship. We've been invited to fellowship with the Most High God, His Son, Jesus, and the Holy Spirit. That's the highest honor that could ever be conferred on us!

Take a moment to get hold of that. You weren't just called to escape hell by the skin of your teeth. You weren't just called to be a church member. You weren't just called to be healed and prosperous. All those things are wonderful, but that's not all He's called you to.

You're called to fellowship with Him, to walk with Him, to talk with Him and to discuss the things of life with Him. In fact, 2 Peter 1:14 says we're called to "participate in the divine nature" *(New International Version)*.

Listen to me. Every believer, I don't care who you are, has the right to hear the voice of the Spirit of the living God. And not shouting at you from off in heaven somewhere, but from right there inside you.

I hear people say, "Well, God's never said anything to me." That's where they're wrong. He's been talking to all of us. He's sent His Spirit to lead us into the truth, and He's been doing His job just fine. The problem is, we haven't spent enough time fellowshiping with Him and listening to Him to hear what He's saying.

We've thought we were fellowshiping

with Him, but most of the time, all we were really doing was having a string of emergency meetings—waiting until a crisis developed and then running to God for an answer.

I used to do that myself. But one time God said to me, *Kenneth, do you realize how much it would mean to Me for you to just come to Me sometimes and say, "Father, I didn't really come today to get anything. I've prayed about my needs already and Your Word says they're met according to Your riches in glory by Christ Jesus. So I just came to be with You. If you have anything You'd like to tell me, I'm ready to listen—and I want You to know that whatever I see in Your Word, I'll do it. I'll put it into effect in my life."*

Most people don't know much about that kind of relationship with God. But the Apostle John calls that fellowship, and he says that kind of relationship with God is what gives us joy (see 1 John 1:3-4).

Emergency praying may give you relief. But fellowship—the intimacy of everyday closeness—is what gives you joy.

One night after a worship service, a friend of mine and I stepped outside and were suddenly awed by the beauty around us. It was one of those crisp, clear winter nights when the brilliance of the moon and stars nearly takes your breath away. I said to my friend, "Tommy, will you look at that!" Then he looked up with one of those Holy Ghost whole-face smiles, and with a voice full of tenderness said, "My Daddy made that!"

"My Daddy...." I'll never forget the way he said that.

Some people might think he shouldn't have been talking in such familiar terms about God. But they'd be wrong. It's scriptural to talk that way about Him. In the New Testament there's an Aramaic word for father: *Abba*. The most accurate translation for that word in English is "Daddy." It's a word that signifies closeness. It speaks of a relationship that's been developed through time spent together.

Father is one thing. Daddy is another.

Growing up, my father was sometimes my father and sometimes my daddy. When we were out duck hunting, he was Daddy. When he gave commands he meant to be obeyed instantly, he was Father.

God is like that too. He's my Father, and He's my Daddy. There are times we're very serious and down to business with one another. Other times we're more lighthearted. *All* the time we belong to one another.

This may come as a surprise to you, but I can tell you from experience that if you'll get to know God and give Him the opportunity, He'll even share His sense of humor with you. He really will. I've had Him say some things to me that cracked me up. But most people don't take the time to develop that kind of fellowship with Him. You see, fellowship is not just relationship. It's beyond that. You can have a relationship without fellowship, but it's like having a marriage without love. The basic structure is there, but the heart of it is missing.

Jesus had more than a relationship with God. They shared the same heart. In Mark 14, there's a gripping picture of the two of them in the Garden of Gethsemane just a few hours before Calvary.

It shows Jesus falling on the ground and praying that if it's possible, the hour ahead might pass from Him. He knows He's about to bear the sin and grief of the whole world. He knows He will be alone, separated from His Father, and He's falling on His face before Him crying out, "Abba." "Daddy, Daddy." It was an incredibly intimate moment.

But here's the amazing thing. According to the Bible, you and I can have that same kind of intimacy with God! In Romans 8:15-16, the Apostle Paul, speaking to believers, says, "For ye have not received the spirit of bondage again to fear; but ye have received the Spirit of adoption, whereby we cry, Abba, Father. The Spirit itself beareth witness with our spirit, that we are the children of God."

Do you hear what I'm telling you? The very same Spirit with which Jesus cried, "Daddy," is the same Spirit with which you cry out to God, "Daddy!"

If you've made Jesus Christ Lord of your life, Jesus is inside you. He's washed you clean by His blood so that now you, too, can cry, "Abba...Daddy!"

I wish I could just pop your head open and stuff this in there until your head and spirit were overflowing with it. God is just as much your Daddy as He is Jesus' Daddy.

You have every ounce as much right to call Him Father as Jesus does because you belong to Jesus.

When I get to thinking about this, I get so excited about it. It's so thrilling to relax in God's presence! Being able to relax in His presence doesn't mean you lose your reverence for Him. In fact, you'll find that as you get to know Him more intimately, your reverence for Him will increase. But instead of being the kind of "reverence" that makes you dodge Him, it will be the kind of reverence that draws you to Him.

Another thing: The more you fellowship with the Father, the more you'll realize how reliable His Word is. Did you know one of the biggest problems people have is coming to grips with the fact that God's Word is 100 percent reliable? It's not difficult to figure out why we have trouble with that. It's because the majority of people have no confidence in their own word.

But the more you fellowship with God around His Word, the more honest and honorable you'll become where your own word is concerned. You'll develop joy. You'll develop faith. You'll start developing

God's own characteristics—just by fellowshiping with Him. You'll begin to understand that you're related to Jesus.

I remember one day I was reading the story of the woman with the issue of blood who touched the hem of Jesus' garment and was healed.

I'd read the story many, many times and pictured myself as almost everybody in the story—just experiencing how it would feel to be someone in the crowd or the one who was healed.

Suddenly God spoke to my spirit and said, *Read that again, and this time picture yourself as the one wearing the garment.*

I was stunned. "Lord," I said, "how can I do that? I can't take Your place!"

That's just what's wrong with the Body of Christ, He told me. *That's the reason the world doesn't know anything about Jesus. You identify with everyone except Me. But I sent you to be MY witnesses, to imitate ME, to stand in MY place—not everybody else's!*

Well, I read it again. This time I pictured myself in the role of the one with the Anointing of the Holy Ghost. Instead of crawling up to touch the hem of His garment, I was the one wearing the garment, freely giving what God had given me.

Once I started reading it like that, I got excited. I wound up reading the rest of the New Testament from that perspective and fellowshiping with Him about it.

Finally I said, "Jesus, I'm beginning to realize how You felt about things when You were here. I'm feeling the compassion You had in You. I'm seeing people, more than ever, through Your eyes. I am beginning to understand more about why You baptized me in Your Holy Spirit."

Not long after that, I found myself in the middle of a group of sick people who wanted to be healed. It didn't feel strange. In fact, it seemed like I'd been there before. Because I'd been fellowshiping with Jesus, all I had to do was just act like Him. I'd already spent time with Him. I'd been learning how He thinks and suddenly it just started coming out of me.

Did you know that's what scares the devil most of all? He knows when you start fellowshiping with the Father, you begin to act like Him. You begin to get strong. And the stronger you get, the more you fellowship with your Father and with your Lord Jesus until He becomes more than just your Savior. He becomes your brother. He becomes your healer. He becomes your financier. He becomes your leader and your guide. Then you get to the place where nothing means more to you than pleasing Him.

It's no wonder the devil wants so desperately to keep you from fellowshiping with God. It's no wonder he'll devise any strategy, any diversion—big or small—to keep you from spending quality time with your Father. He knows that only by interrupting that fellowship can he even begin to get a foothold in your life.

I've seen proof of that over and over again. In my own life, I've discovered that when I fail to fellowship with God, my Word level starts slipping and I begin to slip back toward that depression and oppression that He originally delivered me from.

What's more, since joy comes from fellowship and Nehemiah 8:10 says, "The joy of the Lord is your strength," when I get preoccupied and neglect my fellowship with God, I get weak.

Let me warn you. It's not enough to be out there doing God's work if you're not giving Him any personal time. That can get you into trouble. I know because I've messed up that way many times.

You see, when God speaks to you to do something, you don't need to get in a big hurry. What you do need to do is fellowship with Him about it. There'll come a time when He'll say, *All right. Now it's time to do it.* Then you can get in a hurry.

Here's the bottom line: You'll never truly know God's will and way for you—you'll never know Him for who He really is—until you learn to fellowship with Him and develop a good friendship with Him, and bless Him with your friendship.

So begin right now. Make the decision that you will be one of those people they call a "Word person." I mean you will put God's Word as first place and final authority in your life.

No matter what the world says, no matter what practicality says, no matter what your feelings say—you will walk with God and make your friendship with Him the most important thing in your life.

That's when things will change for you. That's when you'll begin to discover that you really like your heavenly Father and that you can relax in His presence.

That's when you'll truly realize that you don't have a spirit of fear anymore, but a spirit of adoption whereby you cry out, "Daddy, Daddy." That's when, with each day that passes, you'll find yourself more and more right at home in the kingdom of God.

The Attacker

Chapter 10

"A soft answer turneth away wrath."
— PROVERBS 15:1

Mac Hammond

Husband Bill and wife Laura are in bed one night, about to fall asleep. But just before they doze off....

Drip...drip...drip...drip....

Laura: "I can't stand it anymore! That dripping is driving me up the wall. When are you ever going to fix it?" (She's been after Bill for weeks about the leaky bathroom faucet.)

Bill: "How am I supposed to have time to fix the faucet when I'm running around doing all your other errands? I spent half the day yesterday driving your mother back home, and the other half just getting back."

Laura: "So now you're complaining about Mother again. All I did was ask you to...."

Meanwhile, husband Bill and wife Laura cannot remember how this argument even got started. (Not much sleep tonight.)

We know that improving our communication skills is important because our relationships with people are God's primary channels of ministry. He is more likely to use our day-to-day relationships—instead of the supernatural—to meet our needs and the needs of others around us. And God's definition of good communication is simply "speaking the truth in love" (Ephesians 4:15).

So speaking the truth in love is the key to building vital relationships, and to keeping the channels of God's blessings open and flowing.

Let's examine one of the three wrong ways we tend to talk to each other—like Bill and Laura. This is a pattern of conversation that can surface when we, or the people we're talking to, are faced with a problem and the pressure is on.

Understanding the wrong ways can help us learn the right way to communicate.

We'll start with the "attacker pattern."

Round One

In the case of Bill and Laura, both of them acted as attackers in their conversation. Laura started the conversation by attacking Bill. Then Bill responded with a counterattack.

People who attack like this in conversations usually have aggressive personalities. They're the kind of people who strike first, and usually for one of two reasons.

First, they are frustrated with a situation and want it to change. So they confront the person they believe is causing the problem. But out of frustration, they end up attacking the person instead of discussing and solving the problem—like Laura did to Bill.

The other reason is: The best defense is a strong offense. Attacker-type people usually respond to an attack with a counterattack.

Whether attacking or counterattacking, we end up violating God's principles of good communication in three ways when we attack each other in our conversations.

First of all, attackers assume the other person is responsible for their problem. And that it's up to the other person to fix it.

But you may be thinking, *What about Laura—didn't she have a good reason for feeling frustrated with Bill? Wasn't he the source of her problem?*

Well, consider this. God's Word says that our contentment and satisfaction are not dependent upon any other human being— they come from within. Our satisfaction comes from our reborn spirit that has the potential for love, joy, peace, patience, etc. But if this fruit is not surfacing in our lives, it's no one's fault but our own.

Second, attackers create a threatening environment that makes it hard for the other person to hear the truth—even if it is spoken. How?

Let's say a woman has a flat tire at night on a lonely stretch of road in a tough neighborhood. A car with tinted windows slowly drives up and a voice says, "Want a ride?"

Now unless that woman recognizes the voice and car as her husband's, her brother's or someone else's she knows, she probably will turn down the offer even though she needs help. Threatening circumstances can distort what we hear and cause us to change our normal response to a situation.

So when attackers come out swinging, they threaten people, making it hard to understand what they're really trying to say. Their attack distorts the conversation, and they end up communicating nothing but threat to the other person.

Finally, when it comes to speaking the truth in love, attackers violate God's principles of love. Because basically, when they attack someone, they're saying, "You're wrong. You're bad. You blew it and I'm ticked off." They're saying that the other person is a whole lot less than what the Bible says they are in Jesus.

Now the things I'm telling you aren't just off the top of my head or out of some psychology book. The Bible talks about all this.

Build 'Em Up—Don't Shoot 'Em Down

Let's look at James 3:2 to learn more about the attacker. "For in many things we offend all. If any man offend not in word, the same is a perfect man, and able also to bridle the whole body."

How do you feel when someone offends you? Don't you feel attacked or threatened?

Well, God says that if we avoid offending or causing someone to feel threatened, then we're a perfect man—we're mature.

Then how do we actually confront someone with a problem and not make them feel offended or threatened?

Let's see how Jesus does it.

We find Jesus confronting the churches in Revelation 2-3 about some problems and the changes they need to make. He does it in a very effective way that we should imitate.

He starts with the church at Ephesus in Revelation 2:2-4: "I know thy works, and thy labour, and thy patience, and how thou canst not bear them which are evil: and how thou hast tried them which say they are apostles, and are not, and hast found them liars: and hast borne, and hast patience, and for my name's sake hast laboured, and hast not fainted. Nevertheless I have somewhat against thee."

He then goes on to tell them what needs to change.

Now look at verses 12-14: "And to the angel of the church in Pergamos write;

These things saith he which hath the sharp sword with two edges; I know thy works, and where thou dwellest, even where Satan's seat is: and thou holdest fast my name, and hast not denied my faith, even in those days wherein Antipas was my faithful martyr, who was slain among you, where Satan dwelleth. But I have a few things against thee."

And again, He goes on to list the changes they need to make.

Do you see Jesus' pattern?

First He acknowledges all the good things they have done—He affirms them. Then He deals with the problems.

Of course this good pattern can also be abused. Don't do this with the attitude, "Well, I really appreciate all those things you did for me today...but let me tell you what's really bugging me...." That misses the mark.

However, you're on target when you consistently tell the people in your day-to-day life that you appreciate them and the good things they do for you. Then, when a problem surfaces and you confront them about a change that needs to be made, they are less likely to feel threatened. Go to them in love and they will have no reason to raise their walls in defense.

Defuse the Bomb!

But what if you're on the receiving end of the attack, like Bill? How can you avoid a no-win situation like we saw between Bill and Laura?

God tells us in a nutshell: "A soft answer turneth away wrath" (Proverbs 15:1).

I got a firsthand picture of this truth one day in a town meeting.

The church I pastor was planning to open a downtown mission to feed the poor. So we attended a town meeting to discuss our plans with local government officials and citizens of that area.

The city was really angry with us. They were sure that we were planning something that wasn't in the city's or citizens' best interest. Our presence downtown threatened them because they imagined all the transients our mission would draw into their neighborhood.

I tried my best to communicate with

them, but they just couldn't hear me. In fact, the more I talked, the angrier they became.

Then it dawned on me…"A soft answer turneth away wrath."

"I'm sorry," I said. "I didn't realize the depth of your feelings in this. I want to assure you that we're not going to pursue the course of action that you're concerned about."

Bang! It was like deflating a balloon. The situation turned around completely.

By the time the meeting was over, people were telling us how glad they were to see us coming into the community. Today, they tell us how blessed they are to have us down there—even the crime rate has dropped to *zip* in that neighborhood.

It started with a fierce attack…and ended with a soft answer.

The issue boils down to this: Do you want to win the argument? Or do you want God's blessing and power to manifest in your relationships?

If you want to avoid discord and divided relationships, then the next time you're on the receiving end of an attack in a conversation, allow God's Spirit to give you a soft answer. It will turn things around.

So that's the attack pattern. It's the Bill-and-Laura type of conversation that surfaces when there's a problem in a relationship. When you see that kind of conversation about to flare up, remember: Your goal is to speak the truth in love. Then...

Attack the problem, not the person—and you won't offend them.

And if you're under attack, speak a soft word—and you'll defuse the bomb.

But don't wait for problems, start telling people today how much you appreciate them (and don't let up)—then they'll really hear you.

God's Word says you're grown up (in Christ) when you can confront and not attack. It's the mark of a mature believer—and it's God's plan of communication for the Body today.

Forgive by Faith— Not Feelings

"Judge not, and ye shall not be judged: condemn not, and ye shall not be condemned: forgive, and ye shall be forgiven."
— LUKE 6:37

Kenneth Copeland

Spiritually speaking, unforgiveness is downright dangerous. It will make your spirit feeble and your prayers ineffective. Unforgiveness will pull the plug on your faith so completely that you won't have enough power to move the molehills in your life—much less the mountains.

Jesus concluded one of His most powerful teachings on faith with these words, "And when ye stand praying, forgive, if ye have aught against any" (Mark 11:25). Jesus didn't say, "When you stand praying, try to forgive if you can." He simply said, "Forgive." Period.

Jesus did not suggest that we forgive. He made forgiveness a command. And it would be unjust for Him to command us to do something we could not do. Therefore, we know it is within our ability to obey His command to forgive—no matter what the circumstances.

Most people don't realize it, but unforgiveness is actually a form of fear. Quite often we don't forgive because we're afraid of getting hurt again. We're afraid we will never recover from the damage someone has done to our lives.

You may feel that way right now. But the truth of the matter is, you can rely on the fact that your God will supply all your needs according to His riches in glory by Christ Jesus (Philippians 4:19). Let the knowledge of the merciful, protective love of God cast out all your fears (1 John 4:18).

Then forgive by faith, not by feelings. Do it the same way you would receive healing or anything else by faith.

First, make a quality decision to act on God's Word.

Second, speak and act in accordance with that decision. Refuse to say anything negative about anyone who has hurt you. Refuse to rehearse in your mind or with your mouth the hurt they have caused you.

Instead, look for opportunities to bless them, both in word and in deed.

Finally, don't be moved by what you feel. Forgiveness isn't an emotion—it's an act of your will. And when your will lines up with the will of God, heaven's choice blessings are yours!

Increase the Amount in Your Marriage Account

Chapter 12

"And the Lord make you to increase and abound in love one toward another."
— 1 THESSALONIANS 3:12

Dennis and Vikki Burke

Marriages are like bank accounts. You can continue to make regular withdrawals only if you first make significant deposits.

A deposit is an action or word that shows how much value a husband or wife places on the relationship. A deposit could be anything from a tender word, a spontaneous touch or a fresh batch of favorite cookies, to performing a household chore.

A withdrawal is an expectation or requirement that draws out of the relationship to meet a personal need—such as being asked to watch the children so your wife can spend an evening with her friends or to spend a weekend alone while your husband goes hunting.

How do you protect your marriage from the emotional bankruptcy that can come from making more withdrawals than deposits? Find out what enriches your relationship in the eyes of your mate, and also find out what are the biggest draws out of that account. It may surprise you.

You'll discover that the greatest deposits are not purchased with money but with personal involvement in the needs, goals and dreams of your mate. And you'll find out how much the difference in our personalities influences the value we place on each other's actions.

You may be buying flowers and paying someone to take care of the lawn thinking those are two big deposits into your marriage, when your wife longs to see you getting personally involved in her everyday world by painting a room or mowing the grass yourself. Your homemade meals and baked desserts for your husband may be a labor of love. But even though your dad preferred homemade treats, you might discover that your husband prefers store-bought desserts. A bigger deposit might be to let him play golf on Saturday mornings.

Obviously, the big deposits your spouse will make into your life will often come at the cost of his or her own preferences and desires. Learn to recognize and appreciate the effort your mate is making to enrich the relationship. The need to draw upon the strengths and resources of your relationship will always exist. So make sure your marriage account has received regular demonstrations of love, sensitivity and gratitude for one another. Then withdrawals can be made from the overflow of those deposits instead of being scratched out from the bottom of a barrel that has already run dry.

The One to Trust

"Wherein God, willing more abundantly to show unto the heirs of promise the immutability of his counsel, confirmed it by an oath: That by two immutable things, in which it was impossible for God to lie, we might have a strong consolation, who have fled for refuge to lay hold upon the hope set before us."
— HEBREWS 6:17-18

Terri Copeland Pearsons

God is not a liar.

That may sound to you like a very basic truth. Yet many people in the Body of Christ today are talking and behaving as if He were.

What may come as an even greater shock to you is the fact that at one time or another, you and I have been among them.

It's true. In church we've nodded our heads up and down and said, "Yes, Amen. God's Word is true." Then we walked outside and came face to face with sickness or some other kind of problem and we've challenged the truth of the Word of God with our thoughts, our words and our actions. We've followed the course of fear instead of simply expecting God to do what He said He would do for us.

Some people would say, "Well, it's not that I thought God was lying. It's just that we can never really know what He is going to do."

Yes, we can! God has told us what He is going to do! He's literally given us His Word on it. Hebrews 6:16-18 puts it this way: "...an oath for confirmation is to them [men] an end of all strife. Wherein God, willing more abundantly to show unto the heirs of promise the immutability of his counsel, confirmed it by an oath: That by two immutable things, in which it was impossible for God to lie, we might have a strong consolation, who have fled for refuge to lay hold upon the hope set before us."

This simply means that men make pledges or contracts in order to settle disputes. In them responsibilities are clearly defined and obligations made. As long as everyone is true to his word, there's no room for questioning what anyone will do.

Well, God gave us His contract. He is true to His Word so there is no room for uncertainty about it.

God will do what He said He will do. You can count on it.

It Isn't Enough to Remember

"But Terri, what about those times when things didn't turn out like the Word says?"

I can tell you this: If something failed, it wasn't the Word of God. Romans 3:3-4 says: "What if some did not believe and were without faith? Does their lack of faith and their faithlessness nullify and make ineffective and void the faithfulness of God and His fidelity [to His Word]? By no means! Let God be found true though every human being is false and a liar" *(The Amplified Bible).*

Everything that has to do with men, everything in this natural world is subject to change, but the Word of God is not. The Word of God is true even when everything else around you is telling you otherwise. But notice the verse says you must let God be true in your life.

To do so, you must settle forever in your heart and mind: There is no fault in God. There's no shadow of turning in Him. There's no weakness or shortcoming in His Word.

You will never catch God in a lie. You will never get in a situation where you exercise faith in God's Word and God fails to keep that Word. Never! The Bible says that God is active and alert, watching over His Word to perform it. (See Jeremiah 1:12, *The Amplified Bible.*)

Understand, however, that it's not enough just to know what the Word says. It must be reality to you—more real than the problem you face.

I faced the truth of that statement. Even though I've experienced His healing power many times in my life, years ago, I found myself in a serious situation where the health of my children was concerned.

I was receiving one bad report after another. Over a long period of time, simple runny noses had become serious diagnoses.

Finally, I had to sit down and ask myself, *Do I believe that Jesus bore my children's sickness and carried their diseases?*

I had to answer, *No. I know it happened, but I don't believe it.*

Then I said to myself, *Well, you're going to!* And I got my Bible out and meditated on 1 Peter 2:24 that says by his stripes we were healed. I chose to believe that God cannot lie, that His Word is true regardless of what my circumstances are telling me. In my mind, I pictured Jesus on the cross with Jeremy and Aubrey's sickness. I also saw Him coming out of the grave victorious over those sicknesses and then giving that victory to us. I did that for two hours. Two hours. Big deal! Yet those two hours changed the course of my children's health.

It's important for you to realize that throughout that time, I had a basic belief that God has healed us all by the stripes of Jesus. But I had been attempting to exercise faith in God's Word based on head knowledge. That is not enough!

That's why Proverbs 4:20-21 says: "My son, attend to my words; consent and submit to my sayings. Let them not depart from your sight; keep them in the center of your heart" *(The Amplified Bible)*.

For that reason, we must constantly center ourselves on God's Word, because it's that Word that produces faith in our hearts. In fact, you cannot deepen your faith in God without deepening your trust in His Word.

It Becomes What You Need

One of the mistakes holding many believers back from trusting the Word is that they think of God's Word as an item or a "thing." But the Bible tells us that Jesus and His Word are the same. John 1 says: "In the beginning was the Word, and the Word was with God, and the Word was God.... And the Word was made flesh, and dwelt among us, (and we beheld his glory, the glory as of the only begotten of the Father,) full of grace and truth" (verses 1, 14).

Think for a moment about that statement: "The Word was made flesh." The world needed Jesus. He is what man had to have. So God's words and the faith that He released in those words became Jesus.

That is a fundamental characteristic of the Word of God. Mixed with faith, it becomes what you need. God's Word will become finances if you're facing shortage. It will become health when you're faced with sickness.

This one point is so important, I'm going to say it again. No matter what situation you may be facing, if you'll go to God's Word in faith, the Word will become what you need.

The Word Is Alive

How can God's Word become one thing for one person and something else for another? Because it is alive!

For the Word that God speaks is alive and full of power [making it active, operative, energizing, and effective]; it is sharper than any two-edged sword, penetrating to the dividing line of the breath of life (soul) and [the immortal] spirit, and of joints and marrow [of the deepest parts of our nature], exposing and sifting and analyzing and judging the very thoughts and purposes of the heart (Hebrews 4:12, *The Amplified Bible*).

The Word of God is full of life. Full! Therefore it administers life wherever it is applied. It doesn't matter how dark and deadly your circumstances may be. There is enough life in God's Word to totally over-whelm all the death that the world, the devil or circumstances can bring you.

Charles Capps likens the Word to a natural seed. (Actually, 1 Peter 1:23 says the Word is "incorruptible [seed]… which liveth and abideth forever"!) Every seed has within it all the DNA required to produce whatever kind of seed it is. If it's a peach seed, all that is required to be a peach tree is in the seed.

In the same way, the Word of God has the supernatural life within it to fulfill the promises of God in your life. You plant it in your heart as a seed, but when it comes up, it produces salvation, prosperity, healing, deliverance—whatever God has said belongs to you!

The Word Is Truth

John 17:17 says, "Thy word is truth." Notice, it doesn't say, "Thy Word is fact." Truth goes beyond facts.

The fact may be that you don't have any money. The fact may be that the doctor said you have an incurable disease. But what does the truth have to say about it?

You see, truth is absolute. Truth doesn't yield. Truth doesn't change. Thus, facts are subject to truth.

It can be a fact that you are sick as can be, but God says you were healed by the stripes of Jesus when He died on the cross. That's the truth. Now you have a choice. You can apply the truth of God's Word to the fact that you're sick and the fact will change. Or you can agree with the fact, and things will stay like they are.

I'll tell you right now, it will be much easier just to agree with the fact because facts scream a lot louder than the Word of God does. God's Word will be quiet—until it starts coming out of your mouth.

But once that Word begins to come out of your mouth in faith, it will be the final word. If it's God's Word about healing, you'll be healed. If it's His Word about prosperity, you'll be prosperous. If it's His Word about deliverance, you'll be delivered.

God has given you His contract. When you do your part by believing, speaking and acting on a heart full of faith, God's Word will come to pass. No circumstance on earth and no demon in hell can stop it.

So forget all those stories you've heard about how so-and-so believed the Word and it didn't work for him. Quit asking questions, and settle it once and for all. God is not a liar.

People will lie. People will change. They'll say one thing today and another tomorrow. People will often fail to keep their promises. But God is the same yesterday, today and forever—and He keeps His Word. Always. Every time. Without fail.

He's the One to trust.

Speaking the Truth in Love

"That ye put off concerning the former conversation the old man, which is corrupt according to the deceitful lusts; And be renewed in the spirit of your mind; and that ye put on the new man, which after God is created in righteousness and true holiness. Wherefore putting away lying, speak every man truth with his neighbor."
— EPHESIANS 4:22-25

Mac Hammond

When you're having a tough day and need some encouragement to get over the hump, does God appear to you in a puffy little cloud of glory and say, "Be thou encouraged, My child"?

Probably not.

How about a dream, a vision or a voice from heaven to lift you out of the doldrums?

Probably not.

Actually, He's more likely to send someone you know to pat you on the back and tell you, "Cheer up! You're doing a good job and you're going to make it."

Or if money is what you need, God could certainly stick His hand out the window of heaven's sufficiency and drop a sack of coins on your head. But it's more likely that someone you know will come by at just the right time and say, "God put it on my heart that you needed this and I'd like to give it to you."

Simply put—God's primary channel for meeting your needs—or anyone else's—is people.

But if you haven't taken time and made the effort to build relationships with the people around you, then you risk cutting off God's channels of ministry to you—and through you.

So how do you keep those channels open? Communication. Good communication.

Get in the Flow!

Your ability to communicate determines the quality of your relationships and accordingly affects the flow of God's ministry into and out of your life.

For example, if a person is secure in your love, God can use you to bring direction or ministry to that person's life. But if you haven't learned to communicate your heart of love, no matter how genuine it may be, it won't do either of you any good. It's as though you never loved them to begin with, and ministry isn't likely to happen.

Communication is the key. It's how we establish and maintain relationships with each other. But you can be certain that communication is not a spiritual gift from God—it's an acquired skill. You have to work at it and work at it. You have to learn how to communicate.

Let's start learning by looking to God's Word and seeing what it takes to develop those relationships that we so desperately need every day of our lives. The kind of relationships that God can use as a channel to pour His blessings into us—and out of us.

The Word clearly defines good communication in Ephesians 4:15-16: "Speaking the truth in love, may grow up into him in all things, which is the head, even Christ: from whom the whole body fitly joined together...."

Good communication is, first of all, "speaking the truth in love."

As we speak truth to one another in a loving way, we grow up into Christ and become perfectly joined together. That is what the Body of Christ is all about— believers building strong, godly relationships by speaking the truth to each other in every situation, and speaking it in a loving way. This keeps the channels of God's ministry to us open and full, flooding our lives with His blessings and overflowing into the people around us.

But let's face it, speaking the truth in love does not happen naturally. Our human flesh wants to do everything but speak the truth— never mind speaking it in a loving way.

Let's go back to Ephesians 4 and look at verses 22-25. "That ye put off concerning the former conversation the old man, which is corrupt according to the deceitful lusts; and be renewed in the spirit of your mind; and that ye put on the new man, which after God is created in righteousness and true holiness. Wherefore putting away lying, speak every man truth with his neighbor."

The most basic challenge of our daily Christian walk is to put off the old man and put on the new one. Our old nature is corrupt and inconsistent with the flow of ministry God wants to bring into and through our life.

Deception's True Color

So how do we put off our old nature and put on the new one? Notice that the entire process is rooted in first putting away lying and speaking truth instead. The most basic tendency of our old fleshly nature is to lie. Whether the lie is bold, black, gray or white, our old man wants to speak anything but the truth.

Speaking the truth is the first step to effective communication.

Now before you get too comfortable in thinking that you're basically an honest person and you've got this "speaking the truth" part down pat, consider this: A recent survey has established that the average person tells about 200 lies a day. These are not necessarily flat-out lies. They can be slight misrepresentations of the truth or exaggerations of the truth. But they're still not the truth. The tendency to shade the truth is there...in our old nature.

Not only do we have our old nature to overcome in speaking the truth, but we also live in a corrupt world which I believe desensitizes us to lies—however "white" they may seem.

Falsehoods rain down on our heads every day through the media, and we're constantly challenged to discern truth from lie. Evidence of disregard for truth is all around us. Banks won't cash an out-of-town check. Stores won't take returned merchandise without a receipt. It seems you have to use two forms of identification to do almost anything these days.

So with our old, lying nature trying to kick up and our society structured to accommodate dishonesty and deception, we have to be all the more determined to focus our attention on the truth and speak only the truth.

What is that truth?

There are two kinds of truth: temporal (natural truth), and spiritual (God's Word). Temporal truth (such as "it's raining") can be measured by circumstantial evidence, while spiritual truth (such as life after death) can only be measured by the Word of God. On those occasions when there seems to be contradiction between the two realms of truth, choose the Word of God. Don't forget that this natural world was created by the Word of God, so as you speak that Word (truth) in love, you can cause circumstantial truth to change—eliminating those points of contradiction.

As believers we base our lives on God's Word. We do that by filling our heads, our hearts and our mouths with the Word of God—leaving no room for lies or deceptions to interfere in our communication and relationships with people. We speak the truth based on God's Word to every person, in every situation.

However, speaking the truth is not enough.

The second step in effective communication is love..."speaking the truth in love."

Throw Down Your Weapons!

Truth alone can be damaging to your

relationships. Like a sharp sword, telling someone the truth can wound, cause pain and even kill your relationship with them.

If your motive for speaking truth to someone is anything but love, or if the way you express it is anything but loving, the truth can hurt them. And that is not at all God's purpose for truth in our relationships, especially when it comes to relationships within the Body of Christ. God intends for the truth to build us up, not tear us down. Yet too often we take up truth as a weapon, intending to cause harm.

So even if you're simply speaking God's Word to someone about a situation, you should speak it in love. Check your motive before you go to someone to tell him a bit of truth. Make sure it's love, because love tempers the truth so that it is not harsh or abrasive.

When you speak the truth in a loving way, it does not sound rude or arrogant. Rather, it becomes easier for people to receive the truth—even when it may seem hard-hitting—because you are presenting it in a nonthreatening way.

Speaking the truth and speaking it in

love are two steps to good communication.

But once we start communicating with each other, how do our day-to-day relationships actually become channels for God's blessings? What are the benefits of good relationships?

Again, let's go back to Ephesians 4:16 and look at the first part of that verse: "From whom the whole body fitly joined together and compacted by that which every joint supplieth, according to the effectual working in the measure of every part."

Here is a picture of the Body of Christ—a network of strong, godly relationships.

Be a Body Builder

As we step into this attitude and habit of speaking the truth to each other in love, we grow up together and become strong in Christ. We get more in touch and more involved with the people around us.

And as needs arise within this network of relationships, God uses us to supply or give what we have—time, money, encouragement, love—to meet the needs that are within our reach. Eventually this process affects the whole Body. By supplying to each other, we supply to the Body.

But here is what I really want you to see.

Paul closes Ephesians 4:16 by saying, "maketh increase of the body unto the edifying of itself in love."

The result of right, godly relationships is increase.

When we enter into these right relationships that we have built by good communication, we increase. We increase in God's love, we increase in His peace, we increase in His joy. In fact, we increase in everything that makes us more closely conformed to the image of Christ. That's true for you individually and for us corporately as the Church.

Why? Because when the Body of Christ is all rightly related, there are more channels of provision coming in and more channels of ministry going out. God's blessings can flow freely.

But notice that the benefits don't stop there.

The final result of all this increase is that we are edified or built-up in love—individually and corporately—which is one of the primary fruits of right relationships.

So if you've been wondering where God's help was when you needed it, it's ok to have a glorious vision of God personally ministering to you from heaven. But take a look around you.

How are your relationships?

The help you've been waiting for may be only an arm's reach away. Get in touch with the people around you and start working on those relationships by:

1. Focusing your attention on God's Word—your source for all truth.

2. Determining that you're going to speak the truth to everyone, and in every situation.

3. And speaking every word with the purpose of love and in a way of love.

When you do, you'll begin to communicate more effectively and develop stronger relationships—relationships that will edify the Body of Christ and allow God's ministry and blessing to flow in the earth today—into you, throughout the Church and around the world.

Unclog Your Blessing Pipe

"When ye stand praying, forgive, if ye have aught against any: that your Father also which is in heaven may forgive you your trespasses."
— MARK 11:25

Jeanne
Caldwell

Have you ever wondered what happened when—although you're a tither and a generous giver, exercising your faith in God's provision—your flow of blessings abruptly stopped?

That happened to Happy and me once. Happy had been hurt by two men who had defrauded him on a contract. All of a sudden, the flow of our finances just stopped. It seemed as though our prayers came back marked "Return to Sender" and our walk with God had hit a dead end. The blessing pipe just seemed to clog.

Happy was saying, "What's going on here?" until the Lord revealed to him the source of the clog—unforgiveness.

You have to forgive those men, the Lord told Happy. *Keep your heart right. Their hearts may not be right, but I'm dealing with you. Keep walking in obedience to My Word. Keep walking in love.*

So, that day, Happy called those two men over to the house and asked them to forgive him for harboring resentment and unforgiveness toward them. The very next Sunday, we were given a fine automobile! It was a wonderful blessing and a specific answer to prayer. We had been believing God for a new car—but we weren't able to receive it until we purged our hearts of unforgiveness. Unforgiveness had blocked the flow of our prosperity.

Spiritual Drain Opener

In Mark 11:25, Jesus tells us to forgive because unforgiveness will hinder our prayers: "When ye stand praying, forgive, if ye have aught against any: that your Father also which is in heaven may forgive you your trespasses."

Unforgiveness hinders our prayer life because it limits our fellowship with God.

By walking in unforgiveness, we are not walking in love as God commanded. Therefore, when we don't forgive, we walk in disobedience—and disobedience will put us out of position to receive from God. Unforgiveness will stand between us and God to keep our blessings from getting to us. Not only will unforgiveness stop our prosperity, it will also keep us from walking in divine health.

I found that out the hard way a few years ago.

For almost four years, I harbored resentment and unforgiveness against two people who had hurt me. I became sick with a spastic colon because of it. But I didn't have revelation knowledge about how unforgiveness affected my body, so I didn't know what to do. I knew I shouldn't feel the way I did about these people, but I didn't know how to change. I thought, *I'll just stay away from them, and everything will be all right.*

But resentment and unforgiveness don't just go away. You have to repent of them. And as you draw closer to God, He'll reveal that to you.

That's what happened to me. As I

studied the Word, I realized I needed to let go of unforgiveness for the sake of my health. So I wrote a letter to the people who had hurt me. I asked them to forgive me for anything I had said or done that had offended them. I felt 50 pounds lighter after I mailed the letter!

But they showed my letter to other people and said, "See, we told you she was the one at fault. We told you...."

Later, someone asked me, "Did you write so-and-so a letter asking them to forgive you?"

"Yes, I did," I said. "How did you know about it?"

She said, "Because they showed the letter to just about everyone."

When I learned how they had acted, I was tempted to allow bitterness to take root again. I was tempted to say, "Those people haven't changed a bit!"

But I didn't.

No, they hadn't changed—but I had. So I refused to take back that resentment. I said, "Well, I can't help how they responded to my request for forgiveness. I am cleansed from my unforgiveness toward them. That bitterness and hurt is out of me, and I will not take it back."

And I haven't taken it back. The problem with my colon cleared up. I am totally healed. Healing was able to flow into me because I purged myself of resentment and unforgiveness.

Flush Out Aught

"But, Jeanne," you may be asking, "isn't this backward? After all, the people who hurt you were the ones at fault. Why did you have to ask them to forgive you? And Happy wasn't the one who defaulted on that contract. Shouldn't those two men have asked forgiveness from him?"

Well, yes, they should have, but that's not the point. Look again at what Jesus said in Mark 11:25: "Forgive, if ye have aught against any." *Aught* means "anything at all." So, as long as Happy held onto feelings of hurt and offense, as long as I harbored resentment and unforgiveness— anything at all—against those people, we were each out of line with God's Word. Disobedience hinders God's blessings.

That's why prosperity and healing couldn't get through to us.

Asking someone who has hurt you to forgive you for harboring resentment and bitterness toward them will not necessarily change them. But it will change you. And that's important because it enables you to cleanse your heart of the bitterness of a broken relationship—even if it's been broken for years, or even if the other person is dead.

I see this happen in people whose problems are caused by bitterness and unforgiveness toward abusive parents. I ministered to one woman whose deceased mother had been very cruel to her as a child. When she realized that unforgiveness toward her mother was the source of the sickness in her body, she was able to forgive her mother and release the bitterness she harbored against her.

Now, obviously, these actions had no effect on the dead mother. And it couldn't change what the mother had done to her in childhood. But the woman herself changed. She was able to shake off the bondage of bitterness about her past and go on with

God because she made the choice to forgive her mother.

On the other hand, another woman was unable to receive the Baptism in the Holy Spirit because she would not let go of unforgiveness toward her abusive parents.

"Letting go of unforgiveness won't change your parents," I told her. "They may never change. But forgiving them will change you. It will allow healing to flow into your body. It will allow you to go forward spiritually, mentally and physically."

She refused, however, to repent of her hatred toward her parents. Consequently, she was unable to advance in her spiritual walk. Unforgiveness hindered her prayers, robbed her of joy and peace, and stopped the rich flow of God's blessings in her life.

Honey, Call the Plumber!

Not only will "hold[ing] anything against anyone" (Mark 11:25, *New International Version)* hinder your prayers as an individual, it will hinder the prayer of agreement between a husband and wife, and clog their blessing pipe as a family. A member of my

Bible study group sent me a testimony of how she and her husband overcame a blockage in the flow of their blessings after I taught on releasing unforgiveness.

"Our house had been on the market for six months," she wrote, "but we received no offers. We had gone to God's Word, agreed in prayer and confessed in faith that the house was sold, but nothing happened.

"On Tuesday night after you taught how unforgiveness could block healing, I asked my husband if unforgiveness might stop the sale of our home. There was a person whom I thought I had forgiven long ago, but whenever that person's name was mentioned, I felt hate rise up in my heart.

"So my husband and I prayed. Finally, I truly forgave that person. I was completely set free of the burden of unforgiveness.

"Our house sold on Thursday! And my hands, which had been broken out with eczema for over a year, immediately healed up!"

Within 48 hours of getting unforgiveness out of her heart, this woman not only received her healing, but she and her husband also received the financial breakthrough they needed.

Breakthroughs like these are available to anyone who makes a decision to let go of unforgiveness. So if prosperity and health haven't been flowing in your life, inspect your spiritual pipeline. If you find it's clogged with bitterness, resentment and unforgiveness, judge yourself and repent. Then apply Mark 11:25: "Whenever you stand praying, if you have anything against anyone, forgive him and let it drop" *(The Amplified Bible)*. You'll stay healthy and blessed when you do!

Let the Victories Begin!

Chapter 16

"Be ye kind one to another, tenderhearted, forgiving one another, even as God for Christ's sake hath forgiven you."
— EPHESIANS 4:32

Kenneth
Copeland

Forgiveness. Lots of people talk about it. But very few actually do it.

Oh they try...and try and try. But trying just doesn't get the job done. You can come around and talk to those "try-ers" years later and they're still carrying around hurts and resentments. They're still saying, "Well, I'm trying to forgive that person, but what they did to me was just so bad that I just haven't been able to do it yet."

That's why the Word of God doesn't say anything about "trying" to forgive. It simply commands us to forgive "one another, even as God for Christ's sake hath forgiven you" (Ephesians 4:32). Since God has never commanded us to do anything without providing us with the ability to do it, we can be sure He has given every believer the power to forgive in any and every situation.

You may think it is hard to forgive. It's not. Nothing you do by the power of God is hard. You can make it hard by messing around trying to do it in your own strength. But if you'll learn to rest in God through faith in His Word, the struggle will disappear.

You see, if you'll trust God's Word, that Word will fight the fight for you in any area of life. You won't have to wrestle your problems to the ground and solve them with your own great willpower. All you'll have to do is open your Bible and start speaking out God's Word about the situation. Release your faith in that Word and it will conquer any problem—including unforgiveness.

That's right! God's Word will fight the fight of forgiveness for you. If you'll find out what God has to say on the subject—and believe it—it will drive unforgiveness completely out of your life.

No Shades of Gray

Now when I say it will drive unforgiveness from your life, you need to understand, I'm not just talking about a major resentment you've been carrying against someone. I'm also talking about those "little" hurts and offenses that cause you to avoid someone. I'm talking about those memories that cause you to treat someone with less warmth and love because they have injured you in some way.

I'm talking about any attitude you have that falls short of the full light and love of God Himself.

Some people don't want to give up those kinds of things. They'll say, "I love God. Glory! Hallelujah! My fellowship with Him is fine. I'm just having a tough time fellowshiping with Sister So-and-So. But after what she did to me, I just can't help it."

According to the Bible, people who say things like that are lying. They're trying to walk in darkness and light at the same time, and 1 John 1 tells us it can't be done: "This then is the message which we have heard of him, and declare unto you, that God is light, and in him is no darkness at all. If we say that we have fellowship with him, and walk in darkness, we lie, and do not the truth" (verses 5-6).

Notice John didn't stutter there. He didn't say, "Well, bless your heart. Unforgiveness is a sin, but I know how hard these things can be sometimes." No, he said bluntly: "If you walk in darkness and say you have partnership with God, you're lying about it."

The sad thing is many Christians who are walking in unforgiveness don't know they're in darkness. They think that because they read their Bible and say "Amen" at church they're in fellowship with God. But a man who does not forgive is hating his brother, and 1 John 2:11 says, "He that hateth his brother is in darkness, and walketh in darkness, and knoweth not whither he goeth, because that darkness hath blinded his eyes."

"I don't hate him," you may say. "I just don't like him very much!"

How far outside of love do you have to go before it can be called hate? As far as God is concerned, just one step outside of love is hate. To Him there are no shades of gray. In His eyes, anything less than love is sin.

Let me show you something that will mark your thinking. We've already read that God is light and in Him is no darkness at all. If you'll look at 1 John 4:8, you'll find that "God is love." Add to that the fact we learned in 1 John 2:11 about hate being darkness. Put that all together and you can paraphrase 1 John 1:5 and say, "This then is the message which we have heard of him, and declare unto you, that God is love, and in Him is no hate at all."

No Whining, Please

What I'm saying is simply this: We need to face up to the fact that we can't walk with God and be even a little unforgiving or a little offended. If we're going to walk with God, we must allow His love to drive out every trace of any kind of unforgiveness.

"But you just don't know how badly they treated me!"

Has God forgiven your sin?

"Yes."

Then you forgive them. Period. End of discussion.

Quit crying and whining about how hurt you are. Maybe you have been mistreated, but if so—get over it! Everybody has been mistreated in some form or another.

The reason I can talk so straight to you about this is that God has already said these things to me. I remember one day when I was moping around at home. I'd just come in from preaching on the road, and it seemed that as soon as I got there I had to start fighting the devil. I was whining around about it when Gloria said something to me I didn't like.

"Oh, she doesn't care about me anyway," I muttered in self-pity.

Right then, the Lord spoke up in my heart and said, *It isn't any of your business whether she cares for you or not. It's your business to care for her.* Then He added something I'll never forget. He said, *I'm the One who cares whether you hurt or not. Your hurts mean everything in the world to Me, but they ought to mean little or nothing to you.*

As a Church we need to learn that today. We need to quit paying so much attention to our own hurts and cast them over on God. We need to take a lesson from the pioneers of the faith. People like Peter and John and those Pentecostal old-timers years ago would walk into the very jaws of hell. They'd go through persecutions that make the things we face look like child's play. They didn't come out crying about how they'd been hurt either. They came out saying, "Glory to God! We're getting an opportunity to suffer for His Name. What a privilege!"

When you have that attitude, it's not hard to forgive because your focus isn't on yourself. It's on God and His purposes, God and His love.

If you really want to discover the secret of real forgiveness, that's where your focus has to be—on God. For as we read earlier, we are instructed to forgive others in the same way, or on the same basis, that God has forgiven us.

Because of the Blood

Just what is the basis for the forgiveness God has extended to us? First John 2:12 tells us He has forgiven us "for his name's sake." In other words, God has put His Name on an agreement. He has given us His oath that, because Jesus poured out His blood and paid the price for sin, all men are forgiven in His sight. He has put His Name to a document which says He has reconciled the whole world to Himself by Jesus the Anointed, and He is no longer holding anyone's sins against him. (See 2 Corinthians 5:18-19.)

Why did God put His Name on that document? Because of the blood of Jesus. God forgives our sin because He honors the blood. He has said, "I will accept any man, any woman, any child from any place in the world regardless of any sin they have committed. I swore it in the blood and I will do it because of My Name."

Romans 3 puts it this way:

> The righteousness of God [right-
> eousness simply means right-stand-
> ing, or being right with God]...is by

faith of Jesus Christ [the Anointed] unto all and upon all them that believe: for there is no difference: For all have sinned, and come short of the glory of God; being justified freely by his grace through the redemption that is in Christ [the Anointed] Jesus: whom God hath set forth to be a propitiation through faith in his blood, to declare his righteousness for the remission of sins that are past, through the forbearance of God (verses 22-25).

Now, according to those scriptures, there are only two requirements for being made the righteousness of God. Number one is to have sinned and fallen short of the glory of God, which we've all done, and number two is to have faith in the blood of Jesus. Verse 26 goes on to say, "that he might be just, and the justifier of him which believeth in Jesus."

Considering our sin, it would be just for God to say to us, "Get out of My sight. What are you doing walking in here wanting to be a part of My family? Look at your mean, ugly self! Who do you think you are wanting to come into My heaven?"

But, praise God, He doesn't consider our sin. He considers the blood of Jesus. He administers justice based on His blood-sworn oath of forgiveness and, because He honors that blood, He justifies us by wiping out all our sin. The Bible says He remembers our sins no more!

Once those past sins are wiped away, if we miss it and sin again, all we have to do is repent and confess our sin. When we do, the Bible says God is faithful and just to forgive us our sin and cleanse us of all unrighteousness. Why does He do that? Is it because now that we're saved and we're acting better, we deserve to be forgiven? No!

Let me tell you, when I sin there is no way in this world I'm going to go before the throne of grace asking God to forgive me on the basis of how many years I've been in the ministry. I'm not going to pull a dumb stunt like that. I'm just going to go in and plead the blood of Jesus, because I know God honors the blood.

I know His blood is even now in the

heavenly holy of holies, along with a copy of the New Testament. The blood that came out of Jesus' veins is contained in that place, ever reminding all of heaven that this New Covenant—every word of it, including God's promise of forgiveness—was made in the blood of God's Lamb.

That's where my faith rests. I don't have to wonder what God is going to do. I don't have to wonder if He's going to forgive me. I know He will because He swore it in the blood of His own Son.

Serious Business

Now, with all that in mind, I want you to think again about the fact that we are to forgive others as God has forgiven us. Can you see what that means? It means that we're to forgive on the same basis that God forgives—the basis of the blood of Jesus.

My forgiving someone doesn't have anything to do with what that person did or didn't do to me. I forgive because of the blood. God honored the blood and forgave me in the face of my sin, so even as He has forgiven me, I forgive you.

173

For me not to forgive would be to dishonor that blood.

This is serious business we're talking about here! When you dishonor the blood of Jesus, you're stepping out from under its protective covering into the devil's territory. You're stepping out into darkness where he can get a shot at you.

I don't know about you, but I don't want to go out there. I don't care what anyone may do to me, I'm not going to let their mistreatment of me push me out into darkness. No, I'm just going to honor the blood, forgive them and keep right on walking in the light. If somebody hits me on one cheek, I'm just going to do what Jesus said— forgive and turn the other cheek.

Some people think if you do that, you'll get the daylights beaten out of you. But they're wrong. If you keep your faith up, when you turn the other cheek, God will protect you from the one who's trying to hit you.

I know a preacher who experienced that. He was witnessing to a member of a New York street gang who was threatening him with a knife. Instead of fighting back, the preacher just kept telling him Jesus loved him. The guy kept swinging that knife, trying to cut that preacher, but every time he tried, a force he couldn't see stopped him short. He literally couldn't touch him.

As a result, that gang member fell down on his knees, received Jesus, and today he is one of the most outstanding evangelists in the world!

Listen, my friend, forgiveness is one of the most powerful forces in existence! To walk in forgiveness is to walk in victory. To the natural mind, it may seem that if you just keep on forgiving and forgiving, people are going to walk all over you. But it won't happen that way!

Just read what Romans 8:36 says: "As it is written, For thy sake we are killed all the day long; we are accounted as sheep for the slaughter." Is that right? Are we sheep for the slaughter? The next verse tells us. It says, "Nay!" *Nay* means no. *No! No! No!* We're not sheep for the slaughter! On the contrary, "In all these things we are more than conquerors through him that loved us" (verse 37).

When you walk in forgiveness, you're walking in love—and love is more powerful than all the hate Satan can muster. Love never fails. Love makes you more than a conqueror.

What does it mean to be more than a conqueror? Here's the best explanation I ever heard: Imagine a heavyweight boxer who works out day after day, sweating, training, preparing for a big fight. The day of the fight comes and he gets into the ring and goes 15 rounds with some guy who's trying his best to beat his brains out.

When he's finished, he aches from one end to the other. Even his hair hurts. But he won the fight, so they hand him his multi-million-dollar prize money.

Then he goes home and his wife says, "Oh, we won! We won!" He says, "Yeah, we did," and hands her the check. He's a conqueror, but she is more than a conqueror. She didn't get hit one time, but she got all the money!

The Hard Part Is Done!

That's what happened to you. Jesus

went into hell itself and suffered the penalty for sin. He became obedient to death. But by the power of the Holy Spirit and the Word of God, He rose up in great conquest and defeated the devil. He made an open show of him.

Then He turned to you and said, "All power has been given unto Me both in heaven and in earth, now you go in My Name. Here's the prize—now take it and go cast out the devil."

You didn't do any of the fighting, but you got all the power. Jesus gave you the keys to the kingdom!

Don't you dare go around whining about how hard it is to forgive someone. It's not hard! Jesus has done the hard part already. He has shed His blood. All you have to do is honor that blood by making a decision to forgive just as God has forgiven you.

You may not feel any different at first, but that doesn't matter. Forgiveness based on the blood of Jesus is an act of your will, not an act of your feelings. Once that decision is made, don't ever turn back on it. If you see the person you've forgiven a few days later and the old, bad feeling knots up in your stomach, don't be discouraged. That's just a symptom of the flesh.

Rebuke it. Say, "No, I refuse to receive that symptom of unforgiveness. I honor the blood of Jesus and I have forgiven that person." Then treat the person as if no wrong had ever been done.

If you'll keep doing that, God's supernatural ability to forget will rise up within you, and that wrong will be wiped from your consciousness. It won't be long until you see that person walking down the street and you actually won't remember they ever did you any harm.

I can tell you from experience, that kind of victory is sweet. You don't have to wait another moment for it either. You don't have to wait until you "feel" better. You don't have to spend another minute in the dark.

Just make the decision now and say, "Lord, forgive me of this anger and hate. Forgive me on the basis of the blood of Jesus and cleanse me by that blood. I commit before You to honor Jesus' blood by forgiving this person of any wrong he has have ever done to me. I release him from my personal judgment.

"Jesus, bless him, heal him and deliver him. I will speak nothing but good over him from this moment on. Lord, You died for him. You have accepted him in Jesus and if he's good enough for You, he's good enough for me. Therefore, I love him completely and without reserve, in Jesus' Name. Amen."

If you just prayed that prayer, rejoice! You're no longer trying to forgive; you've done it. You've stepped out of darkness into the Light. You've hooked into the supernatural, never-failing power of love.

So shout hallelujah—and let the victories begin!

Prayer for Salvation and Baptism in the Holy Spirit

Heavenly Father, I come to You in the Name of Jesus. Your Word says, "Whosoever shall call on the name of the Lord shall be saved" (Acts 2:21). I am calling on You. I pray and ask Jesus to come into my heart and be Lord over my life according to Romans 10:9-10: "If thou shalt confess with thy mouth the Lord Jesus, and shalt believe in thine heart that God hath raised him from the dead, thou shalt be saved. For with the heart man believeth unto righteousness; and with the mouth confession is made unto salvation." I do that now. I confess that Jesus is Lord, and I believe in my heart that God raised Him from the dead.

I am now reborn! I am a Christian—a child of Almighty God! I am saved! You also said in Your Word, "If ye then, being evil, know how to give good gifts unto your children: HOW MUCH MORE shall your heavenly Father give the Holy Spirit to them that ask him?" (Luke 11:13). I'm also asking You to fill me with the Holy Spirit. Holy Spirit, rise up within me as I praise God. I fully expect to speak with other tongues as You give me the utterance (Acts 2:4). In Jesus' Name. Amen!

Begin to praise God for filling you with the Holy Spirit. Speak those words and syllables you receive—not in your own language, but the language given to you by the Holy Spirit. You have to use your own voice. God will not force you to speak. Don't be concerned with how it sounds. It is a heavenly language!

Continue with the blessing God has given you and pray in the spirit every day.

You are a born-again, Spirit-filled believer. You'll never be the same!

Find a good church that boldly preaches God's Word and obeys it. Become a part of a church family who will love and care for you as you love and care for them.

We need to be connected to each other. It increases our strength in God. It's God's plan for us.

Make it a habit to watch the *Believer's Voice of Victory* television broadcast and become a doer of the Word, who is blessed in his doing (James 1:22-25).

Books Available From
Kenneth Copeland Ministries

by Kenneth Copeland

* A Ceremony of Marriage
  A Matter of Choice
  Covenant of Blood
  Faith and Patience—The Power Twins
* Freedom From Fear
  Giving and Receiving
  Honor—Walking in Honesty, Truth and Integrity
  How to Conquer Strife
  How to Discipline Your Flesh
  How to Receive Communion
  In Love There Is No Fear
  Know Your Enemy
  Living at the End of Time—A Time of Supernatural Increase
  Love Never Fails
  Mercy—The Divine Rescue of the Human Race
* Now Are We in Christ Jesus
  One Nation Under God (gift book with CD enclosed)
* Our Covenant With God
  Partnership, Sharing the Vision—Sharing the Grace
* Prayer—Your Foundation for Success
* Prosperity: The Choice Is Yours
  Rumors of War
* Sensitivity of Heart
* Six Steps to Excellence in Ministry
* Sorrow Not! Winning Over Grief and Sorrow
* The Decision Is Yours
* The Force of Faith
* The Force of Righteousness
  The Image of God in You
* The Laws of Prosperity
* The Mercy of God (available in Spanish only)

*Available in Spanish

by Gloria Copeland

The Protection of Angels
There Is No High Like the Most High
The Secret Place of God's Protection (gift book with CD enclosed)
The Unbeatable Spirit of Faith
This Same Jesus
To Know Him
Walk With God
Well Worth the Wait
Words That Heal (gift book with CD enclosed)
Your Promise of Protection—The Power of the 91st Psalm

Books Co-Authored by Kenneth and Gloria Copeland

Family Promises
Healing Promises
Prosperity Promises
Protection Promises

* From Faith to Faith—A Daily Guide to Victory
From Faith to Faith—A Perpetual Calendar

One Word From God Can Change Your Life

One Word From God Series:
• One Word From God Can Change Your Destiny
• One Word From God Can Change Your Family
• One Word From God Can Change Your Finances
• One Word From God Can Change Your Formula for Success
• One Word From God Can Change Your Health
• One Word From God Can Change Your Nation
• One Word From God Can Change Your Prayer Life
• One Word From God Can Change Your Relationships

Load Up—A Youth Devotional
Over the Edge—A Youth Devotional
Pursuit of His Presence—A Daily Devotional
Pursuit of His Presence—A Perpetual Calendar

*Available in Spanish

Raising Children Without Fear

Other Books Published by KCP

Real People. Real Needs. Real Victories.
    A book of testimonies to encourage your faith
John G. Lake—His Life, His Sermons, His Boldness of Faith
The Holiest of All by Andrew Murray
The New Testament in Modern Speech by Richard Francis Weymouth
The Rabbi From Burbank by Rabbi Isidor Zwirn and Bob Owen
Unchained! by Mac Gober

Products Designed for Today's Children and Youth

And Jesus Healed Them All (confession book and CD gift package)
Baby Praise Board Book
Baby Praise Christmas Board Book
Noah's Ark Coloring Book
The Best of *Shout!* Adventure Comics
The *Shout!* Giant Flip Coloring Book
The *Shout!* Joke Book
The *Shout!* Super-Activity Book
Wichita Slim's Campfire Stories

*Commander Kellie and the Superkids*_{SM} Books:

The SWORD Adventure Book
*Commander Kellie and the Superkids*_{SM} Solve-It-Yourself Mysteries
*Commander Kellie and the Superkids*_{SM} Adventure Series:
    Middle Grade Novels by Christopher P.N. Maselli:

    #1 The Mysterious Presence
    #2 The Quest for the Second Half
    #3 Escape From Jungle Island
    #4 In Pursuit of the Enemy
    #5 Caged Rivalry
    #6 Mystery of the Missing Junk

World Offices of
Kenneth Copeland Ministries

For more information about KCM and a free
catalog, please write the office nearest you:

Kenneth Copeland Ministries
Fort Worth, Texas 76192-0001

Kenneth Copeland
Locked Bag 2600
Mansfield Delivery Centre
QUEENSLAND 4122
AUSTRALIA

Kenneth Copeland
Post Office Box 15
BATH
BA1 3XN
U.K.

Kenneth Copeland
Private Bag X 909
FONTAINEBLEAU
2032
REPUBLIC OF
SOUTH AFRICA

Kenneth Copeland
PO Box 3111 STN LCD 1
Langley BC V3A 4R3
CANADA

Kenneth Copeland Ministries
Post Office Box 84
L'VIV 79000
UKRAINE

We're Here for You!

Believer's Voice of Victory Television Broadcast

Join Kenneth and Gloria Copeland and the *Believer's Voice of Victory* broadcasts Monday through Friday and on Sunday each week, and learn how faith in God's Word can take your life from ordinary to extraordinary. This teaching from God's Word is designed to get you where you want to be—*on top!*

You can catch the *Believer's Voice of Victory* broadcast on your local, cable or satellite channels.

Check your local listings for times and stations in your area.

Believer's Voice of Victory Magazine

Enjoy inspired teaching and encouragement from Kenneth and Gloria Copeland and guest ministers each month in the *Believer's Voice of Victory* magazine. Also included are real-life testimonies of God's miraculous power and divine intervention in the lives of people just like you!

It's more than just a magazine—it's a ministry.

To receive a FREE subscription to *Believer's Voice of Victory,* write to:

Kenneth Copeland Ministries
Fort Worth, Texas 76192-0001
Or call:
(800) 600-7395
(7 a.m.-5 p.m. CT)
Or visit our Web site at:
www.kcm.org

If you are writing from outside the U.S., please contact the KCM office nearest you. Addresses for all Kenneth Copeland Ministries offices are listed on the previous pages.